A Citizen's Guide to U.S. Foreign Policy: Election '88

Prepared by the Editors of
the Foreign Policy Association
New York, New York

This publication has been underwritten by a major grant from Philip Morris Companies Inc.

All rights reserved. No part of this book may be reproduced or transmitted in any form or by any means, electronic or mechanical, including photocopying, recording or by any information storage and retrieval system, without permission in writing from the publisher.

Published by the Foreign Policy Association
Chairman: Robert V. Lindsay
President: John W. Kiermaier
Editor in Chief: Nancy L. Hoepli
Senior Editors: Susan Zelony Breen, Nancy King, Ann R. Monjo and Lawrence G. Potter
Special Projects Editor: K.M. Rohan
Editorial Assistant: Alexandra Dubow
Editorial Interns: Cecilia Ciepiela, Ana Maria Harkins, Jane M. Hughes, Austin Denis Johnston, Anthony C. Paspatis, Andrew M. Rosen, Lynn D. Waddell and Efrot Weiss
Consultants: C. Michael Aho, Christopher A. Kojm and J. Owen Zurhellen, Jr.

Typography and design: K.M. Rohan

© Copyright 1988 by the Foreign Policy Association, Inc.
729 Seventh Avenue, New York, N.Y. 10019

Printed in the United States of America
Library of Congress Card Number: 88-81554
ISBN: 0-87124-119-6

BOMC offers recordings and compact discs, cassettes and records. For information and catalog write to BOMR, Camp Hill, PA 17012.

CONTENTS

Leadership
1. President, Congress and Foreign Policy 5

Security
2. Controlling the Arms Race 12
3. Defense: How Much Is Enough? 22
4. Dealing with Terrorism 32

Economic and Social Issues
5. Trade, the Dollar and Foreign Investment 39
6. Foreign Aid and the Third World 48
7. International Drug Traffic 57

Critical Regions
8. Central America 63
9. Middle East Flash Points 73
10. Southern Africa in Turmoil 84
11. The Atlantic Alliance 93
12. South Asia: India and Pakistan 101

Bilateral Relations
13. Gorbachev's Soviet Union 109
14. Canada: A Good Neighbor 118
15. Mexico in Transition 125
16. China and Taiwan 134
17. Japan: Economic Colossus 141

United Nations
18. The U.S. and the UN 147

Index 155

FOREWORD

As voters prepare to choose a President, the Foreign Policy Association, a private, nonprofit, nonpartisan educational organization, has prepared this small volume on some of the most difficult foreign policy issues facing the next Administration. FPA's objective throughout its 70 years has been to help stimulate an informed, thoughtful and articulate public opinion. It does so through its publications, its sponsorship of nationwide discussion groups and foreign affairs programs for all interested Americans.

This citizen's guide is one of a series produced by the Foreign Policy Association in every presidential election year since 1968. The guide's purpose is to provide the general voter, officeholders, candidates, students and teachers with the background information they need to take part in the national foreign policy debate and reach their own informed conclusions. FPA is convinced that if citizens have access to the facts, no issue is so complex that they cannot understand it. And, by their votes and voices, they will ultimately decide the course of U.S. foreign policy.

FPA is proud that the Book-of-the-Month Club has chosen this guide as a pro bono gift to its members.

We are also most grateful to Philip Morris for their grant, which has allowed the editors of FPA to produce a comprehensive citizen's guide of quality.

John W. Kiermaier
President of FPA

1

President, Congress and Foreign Policy

✔ *What is Congress' proper role in making foreign policy?*

✔ *In the wake of the Iran-contra affair, should policymaking be reformed?*

✔ *What guidelines for a post-Reagan foreign policy?*

BACKGROUND

The President and Congress. The power to make foreign policy is divided under the Constitution. The President sets policy, but the Congress controls the "power of the purse" and can withhold funds for carrying out presidential initiatives. The President is commander in chief of the armed forces, but only Congress can declare war. The Senate's consent is necessary for the President to approve treaties and appoint ambassadors. Historically, the pendulum of power has swung back and forth between Presidents and Congress, with a strong executive prevailing throughout most of this century. This division of power in foreign-policy making in the U.S. often confuses other countries.

The creation of the National Security Council (NSC) and the Central Intelligence Agency (CIA) in 1947 contributed to policy fragmentation within the executive branch. The NSC, set up to help the President coordinate security policy, consists of the President, Vice President and secretaries of State and Defense. (The Chairman of the Joint

Chiefs of Staff and the Director of Central Intelligence serve as advisers.) The NSC staff is headed by the assistant to the President for national security affairs. In recent years, strong national security advisers have vied with the Secretary of State for influence over policy, often successfully. The CIA at times has also had a major role in policymaking. Disclosures in the 1970s that the CIA had spied on U.S. citizens at home and had been involved in attempted coups d'état and assassination plots abroad led to stricter congressional monitoring of intelligence activities and a cutback of funds and staff.

Breakdown of consensus. The postwar consensus on foreign policy, based on containing communism and promoting democracy, eroded during the Vietnam War. Many Americans were disillusioned by foreign adventures, and a new isolationism set in. Congress, believing flawed policies had led to defeat in Vietnam, reasserted its role in policymaking. Swelling congressional staffs, assisted by nonpartisan agencies such as the General Accounting Office, the Congressional Budget Office and the Congressional Research Service, gave Congress greater expertise to question Administration policies and frame alternatives.

In the post-Vietnam backlash, Congress sought to curb presidential power. The most notable restriction was the War Powers Resolution, which attempted to check the President's ability to make war. (The last time Congress declared war was World War II.) The resolution was enacted in 1973 over President Richard M. Nixon's veto. He and subsequent Presidents have maintained it is unconstitutional. The resolution requires the President to notify Congress within 48 hours of introducing troops into a hostile situation abroad, and to withdraw them within 60 to 90 days unless Congress authorizes a longer stay.

The Reagan revolution. In Ronald Reagan's first term, Congress generally supported the Administration's foreign policy. It voted major budget increases for both defense and intelligence. Central America was another matter: the Democratic majority in Congress and public opinion did not share the Administration's view that the leftist Sandinista government in Nicaragua was a threat to U.S. national security. A series of amendments to the defense authorization bill, named for their cosponsor, Rep. Edward P. Boland (D-Mass.), placed restrictions on U.S. aid to the Nicaraguan resistance starting in 1982. The third and most sweeping version of the Boland Amendment, in effect from Oct. 1984 to Sept. 1985, barred all aid to the contras, humanitarian as well as military (see Chapter 8).

State's budget cut. The 1985 Gramm-Rudman-Hollings deficit-reduction legislation, prompted by a swelling Federal deficit, forces the government to achieve a balanced budget by 1991. The budget for foreign affairs, including funds for the State Department and foreign aid, has been cut sharply in the past three years. In fiscal year (FY) 1985, the foreign affairs budget totaled $26.5 billion, $20.2 billion of which went for foreign aid. The figures for FY 1988 (ending Sept. 30) were $17.7 billion and $13.97 billion, respectively. This continues a decades-long trend: in the early 1950s, 10% of the Federal budget was devoted to international affairs; by the mid-1960s, 5%; and currently, less than 2%. In 1988 State's budget was only increased 2%, although it needed a 10.5% boost to maintain current program levels.

To economize, the department let go many of the Foreign Service's most experienced middle-level diplomats in their late 40s and early 50s. Generalists with managerial experience are being given priority in promotion over specialists in critical areas and languages. Critics claim the U.S. is depriving itself of expertise at a time of growing need in today's complex world.

Legacy. In its last two years in office, part of the Administration's energies were consumed by the Iran-contra affair, part in trying to leave a record of accomplishments. The major achievement was the Dec. 1987 agreement with the Soviet Union to ban intermediate-range nuclear forces, or INF (see Chapter 2). The treaty was overwhelmingly approved by the Senate in May 1988.

The Iran-contra affair grew out of the Administration's preoccupation with freeing U.S. hostages in the Middle East (see Chapter 9). According to investigations by a joint congressional panel and a review board appointed by the President (the Tower Commission), members of the NSC staff (national security advisers Robert C. McFarlane and Vice Adm. John M. Poindexter, assisted by Lt. Col. Oliver L. North), working with the late CIA director William J. Casey, secretly sold arms to Iran to obtain the release of Americans held hostage in Lebanon. They did so in violation of official U.S. policy prohibiting negotiating with terrorists and selling arms to Iran. The deals were also intended to bolster "moderates" in Iran and lead to a warming of U.S. relations with that country. Some of the funds from the arms sales were diverted to the contras in violation of the Boland Amendment.

Executive struggles. The investigations threw a spotlight on how the executive branch made foreign policy. The NSC staff had "privatized" foreign policy: they hired private citizens and foreign middlemen to carry out actions directly contrary to policies espoused by the State and Defense departments. Top U.S. military commanders as well as the Secretary of State were excluded from the secret initiatives. Congressional oversight was circumvented and intelligence information was skewed to support the secret policies. The result was to call into question the credibility of American foreign policy.

Secretary of State George P. Shultz complained of a battle royal being waged for the ear of the President, and noted that, even after policies were adopted, the losing side never gave up the fight to have them reversed. "Nothing ever gets settled in this town," Shultz said.

Leadership

Wasserman © 1986, *The Boston Globe*.

The revelations of the Iran-contra affair portrayed a President out of touch on crucial issues and made competence and experience key issues in the 1988 presidential race. While many criticized President Jimmy Carter for being too involved in the minutiae of policy, they felt Reagan was not involved enough.

Foreign policy for the 1990s. Some analysts believe the postwar era of international relations has ended and there is a need to bring the nation's commitments and resources into balance. U.S. economic strength has eroded, they claim, and reducing the U.S. budget deficit is a key priority for a sustainable foreign policy. They believe the U.S. can no longer afford maintaining large military commitments around the world. (At the end of 1987, the U.S. had 520,000 soldiers and 65,000 sailors stationed abroad and had major bases in Japan, the Philippines, South Korea, West Germany, Greece, Turkey, Spain and Portugal.) Dangerous also is the American dependence on foreign capital—especially Japanese.

Others argue that postwar U.S. policy has assured general political stability, with no major wars and significant economic advances. They point out that the U.S. is still the most powerful country in the world, militarily and economically, and that American democracy is much admired. In contrast, they note, Marxism-Leninism seems to have lost its appeal in the Third World. They believe that part of the solution to the economic burden of U.S. commitments is for U.S. allies to assume a greater share of defense spending.

POLICY CHOICES

❏ The State Department, not the NSC, should conduct foreign policy.
Yes. (1) The Secretary of State is charged with carrying out foreign policy, and, unlike the national security adviser, he is subject to confirmation by the Senate. (2) The State Department, unlike the small NSC staff, is run predominantly by career Foreign Service officers trained in the conduct of foreign policy.
No. (1) The NSC advises the President on national security policy after considering the interests of all executive agencies, not just the State Department. (2) The State Department is a large, unwieldy and slow-moving bureaucracy, with its own vested interests, which are not necessarily shared by the President.

❏ The President should accept the War Powers Resolution.
Yes. (1) By unilaterally committing U.S. forces abroad, Presidents have ignored the constitutional power of Congress to declare war. (2) By invoking the War Powers Resolution, the President enables Congress to voice support for his policy, thereby strengthening it.
No. (1) The act is unconstitutional and unfairly ties the President's hands. (2) It puts the U.S. at a disadvantage vis-à-vis its foreign adversaries by giving them advance notice of restrictions on U.S. power.

☐ The State Department budget should be increased.
Yes. This is necessary to enable the U.S. to carry out its expanded global responsibilities.
No. There can be no exceptions in the drive to reduce the Federal deficit, which is essential to this country's present and future economic well-being.

SELECT BIBLIOGRAPHY

Deibel, Terry L., "Presidents, Public Opinion and Power: The Nixon, Carter and Reagan Years." *Headline Series* No. 280. New York, Foreign Policy Association, Apr. 1987. Suggests elements of a post-Reagan foreign policy.

Fundamentals of U.S. Foreign Policy. Washington, D.C., U.S. Department of State, Bureau of Public Affairs, Mar. 1988. 97 pp. Addresses the interests and objectives of U.S. foreign policy.

Gilpin, Robert, "American Policy in the Post-Reagan Era." *Daedalus,* Summer 1987, pp. 33–67. As the postwar era of international relations ends, U.S. policy must adjust.

Huntington, Samuel P., "Coping with the Lippmann Gap." *Foreign Affairs,* Vol. 66, No. 3 *(America and the World 1987/88),* pp.453–77. Steps the U.S. should take to reduce the gap between commitments and capabilities.

Kennedy, Paul, "The (Relative) Decline of America." *The Atlantic Monthly,* Aug. 1987, pp. 29–38. The economic decline of the U.S. calls for a reduced global role.

2
Controlling the Arms Race

✔ *What kind of arms control agreements should the U.S. pursue?*

✔ *Has the time come to stop all nuclear tests?*

✔ *Should the U.S. make concessions in order to reach agreements? Should it hang tough?*

BACKGROUND

Since the beginning of the nuclear age in 1945, the U.S. has participated in many arms control negotiations. Between 1945 and 1957, as the U.S. sought to retain its nuclear advantage and the Soviet Union sought to catch up, both countries aired broad proposals for stopping the arms race, but there was little basis for agreement. In the meantime, both sides expanded their arsenals. As Soviet nuclear weapons development brought the superpowers closer to parity over the next two decades, Washington and Moscow began finding common ground for agreement: a shared interest in reducing levels of radioactive fallout from weapons testing, checking the other's arms production and technological advances, and above all avoiding a nuclear war.

The goals advanced for arms control over the years include:

• freezing or reducing the number of nuclear weapons,

• lowering the economic costs of the arms race,

• advancing the process of communication and cooperation between the superpowers,

- bringing *stability* to the nuclear arms competition, by making sure each side's forces are structured so that the other is deterred from using its nuclear weapons or threatening to use force in order to gain a political or military objective; making the other side's weapons development decisions more predictable; and making sure neither side ever has an incentive to strike first.

Major bilateral arms control agreements:

■ **1963 "hot-line" accord,** providing rapid, reliable communication between the superpowers (the communication links established were upgraded in 1971, 1978 and 1984);

■ **1963 limited test ban treaty,** ending all but underground nuclear tests;

■ **1971 "accidents measures" agreement,** requiring both superpowers to add technical and organizational safeguards against the accidental or unauthorized launch of nuclear weapons, and providing for notification of the other side in case of accidental or unauthorized use;

■ **1972 SALT I (strategic arms limitation talks) agreement,** consisting of:

Treaty on antiballistic missile systems (ABM), which limited ABM deployment to two sites in each country, subsequently reduced to one. An agreed statement appended to the treaty provided for discussions in the event that new "ABM systems based on other physical principles" were developed. The treaty was of unlimited duration.

Interim agreement on the limitation of strategic offensive arms, which froze the number of land- and sea-based ballistic missile launchers and banned the replacement of older missiles with significantly heavier ones for five years. The U.S. agreed to a freeze at unequal levels (2,347 for the U.S.S.R., 1,710 for the U.S.) as part of a compromise: the U.S.S.R. insisted on numerical compensation for what it claimed were U.S. technological and geographical advantages. The agreement also permitted verification through the use of "national technical means" (satellite reconnaissance and radar and electronic surveillance).

- **1974 threshold test ban treaty,** prohibiting underground weapons tests with yields of over 150 kilotons, and its companion, the **1976 peaceful nuclear explosions treaty,** limiting underground nuclear tests for peaceful purposes. (Although the Carter Administration favored both, the Senate never ratified either. The Reagan Administration has opposed ratification until verification provisions are strengthened.)
- **1979 SALT II agreement,** setting equal ceilings (2,400) on numbers of launchers on both sides, as agreed at the 1974 Vladivostok summit meeting between President Gerald R. Ford and Soviet leader Leonid I. Brezhnev. A ceiling of 1,320 was set for multiple warhead launchers; a freeze was placed on throw-weight; and the number of warheads permitted on any intercontinental ballistic missile (ICBM) was limited to 10. Further subceilings were agreed on for numbers of launchers with multiple independently targetable reentry vehicles (MIRVs). The treaty was never ratified by the Senate, but both the U.S. and U.S.S.R. agreed to abide by its provisions as well as those of the SALT I interim agreement (which expired in 1977). The Reagan Administration repeatedly questioned Soviet compliance with the treaty, and deliberately exceeded SALT II limits in 1986. It subsequently agreed to abide by a new informal limit on multiple warheads (1,345), set by Congress as part of a compromise defense funding agreement in Nov. 1987.
- **1987 "nuclear risk reduction centers" (NRRCs) agreement,** committing both sides to work toward improving the constant communications between Washington and Moscow set up by the hot-line and accidents measures agreements.
- **1987 INF (intermediate-range nuclear forces) treaty,** which will eliminate all U.S. and Soviet nuclear weapons with ranges between 300 and 3,400 miles. Under the agreement, the U.S. will destroy 859 missiles, the U.S.S.R., 1,752. This is the first agreement that reduces, rather than sets ceilings on, numbers of nuclear weapons.

Current negotiations:

■ **Strategic arms reduction talks** (START). The Reagan Administration dropped SALT in favor of START in an attempt to achieve reductions of, rather than only setting limits to, levels of strategic weapons. After a four-year stalemate, negotiations in 1986–87 led to the signing of the INF treaty and gave impetus to the START talks. President Ronald Reagan hopes to sign an agreement with Soviet leader Mikhail Gorbachev on strategic weapons before he leaves office, based on a formula worked out at the 1986 Reykjavik, Iceland, summit, that would reduce numbers of strategic weapons on both sides by 50%, leaving each side with 6,000 warheads on a maximum of 1,600 launchers. Agreement was reached at the Dec. 1987 summit in Washington that, of the 6,000 warheads, 4,900 could be on ballistic missiles and of these, 1,540 could be launched from "heavy" (large, multiwarhead) land-based ICBMs. The Soviet Union has also agreed to cut the total throw-weight of its arsenal by 50%.

Before such a treaty can be signed, a number of issues need to be resolved:

Strategic Defense Initiative (SDI) and the ABM treaty. The Reagan Administration has interpreted the ABM treaty to give it the right to develop and test new SDI technology which is based on "other physical principles" from those available at the time the ABM treaty was signed. Administration critics and Moscow disagree with this interpretation, and in Oct. 1987 the Administration reached a compromise with Congress to abide by the more restrictive interpretation of the ABM treaty for one year. Moscow wants the U.S. to adhere to the narrow interpretation for 10 years; the Administration will only agree to a seven-year commitment, and then only to the broad interpretation. Moscow has repeatedly warned that it will not consider itself bound by any treaty on strategic arms if the U.S. violates the Soviet understanding of the ABM treaty.

What should be cut? The U.S. wants to see an

additional sublimit of 3,300 on land-based ICBMs, which it considers the Soviet's greatest strength and greatest threat to stability. The Soviet Union has countered with a demand for a sublimit of 1,800 to 2,000 on submarine-launched ballistic missiles (SLBMs), in which the U.S. is stronger. Washington and Moscow also disagree over limits on air-launched cruise missiles, on the Backfire bomber and on aspects of verification.

■ **Conventional arms talks: Mutual and Balanced Force Reductions (MBFR).** Since 1973 the North Atlantic Treaty Organization (NATO) and the Soviet-East European military alliance, the Warsaw Pact, have held inconclusive talks on reducing conventional forces in Central Europe. The main obstacle has been a dispute over the number of active-duty Warsaw Pact troops in the reduction area. In June 1986, the Soviet Union proposed new negotiations on force reductions over a much wider area, "from the Atlantic to the Urals" (see map). Gorbachev called for immediate cuts by both sides of 100,000 to 150,000 men, and 500,000 by the early 1990s. Gorbachev has also acknowledged that there is a "certain asymmetry, both in forces and armaments," in Central Europe, and hinted that the Warsaw Pact might be prepared to make one-sided reductions. Moscow suggested that its new proposal could be negotiated in new talks, in an expanded MBFR framework, or else in a second round of the Conference on Disarmament in Europe (CDE). (The 35-nation CDE talks were held from 1984 to 1986 in Stockholm, Sweden. They led to agreement in Sept. 1986 on a series of confidence-building measures to reduce the danger of surprise attack in Europe, including advance notification of major military maneuvers and on-site verification measures to ensure compliance.)

In late 1987, NATO proposed that the U.S.S.R. unilaterally cut 50% of its tanks and artillery in order to bring Warsaw Pact levels into balance with those of the Atlantic alliance. Moscow attacked the plan as unfair because it made no mention of what Moscow believes are imbalances in NATO's favor, such as in tactical aircraft.

The new approach may prove more negotiable than the old one. NATO and Warsaw Pact forces are more evenly balanced in the larger zone. In the MBFR area, Warsaw Pact forces outnumbered NATO by about 200,000 (an advantage the Soviets never explicitly acknowledged); in the new area, NATO has an advantage of about 90,000, because of the addition of troops from Spain, Portugal, Denmark, Norway, France, Italy, Greece and Turkey, plus British and American forces in Britain and U.S. forces in Iceland. (Hungary, Bulgaria and Romania would be counted on the Warsaw Pact side.) On the other hand, getting such a large number of Western countries—not all of whose troops are integrated into the NATO military command structure—to agree on all is-

Area Covered by CDE Agreement

The Stockholm agreement signed in Sept. 1986 provides for confidence-building measures and covers all of Europe, from the Atlantic Ocean to the Ural Mountains of the Soviet Union. The 35 participants include the United States, Canada and all European nations except Albania.

Area Covered by MBFR Negotiations

MBFR negotiations concern troop levels and armaments in the territory of East Germany, Poland, Czechoslovakia, West Germany, Belgium, the Netherlands and Luxembourg. Participants include the seven nations whose territory is involved, and the United States, Canada, Britain and the Soviet Union. MBFR talks have continued since 1973 without reaching an agreement.

sues may be difficult. Another advantage for NATO in an Atlantic-to-Urals agreement is that Soviet forces would have to be pulled back much further than the several hundred miles required under the old MBFR formula. The new talks would also focus on reducing numbers of weapons rather than numbers of troops, which experts believe will make counting easier.

Tricky issues to resolve include **tactical (battlefield) nuclear weapons** (with a range of less than 300 miles): Moscow wants to include them in the talks, and the U.S. does not. The U.S. also does not want to discuss limits on dual-capable **aircraft** (aircraft that can carry either nuclear or conventional weapons) in Europe. Other problems pertain to how limits would be set: Would there be collective ceilings for each alliance or individual ceilings for individual countries? Moscow has generally preferred the latter, which the U.S. has resisted. The size of American and Soviet forces within the reduction zone would also pose problems, since the Atlantic-to-Urals area includes Soviet territory—and therefore the U.S.S.R.'s 1.8 million troops. (The U.S. has approximately 350,000 troops in Europe.)

■ **Test ban.** The Soviet Union declared a unilateral moratorium on all testing of nuclear weapons in Feb. 1985, which it broke following a U.S. test in Feb. 1987. Moscow is still pushing for a comprehensive ban on all underground testing. In the U.S., Democratic presidential candidates Michael Dukakis and Jesse Jackson favor negotiating such a ban as well as a ban on all flight testing of ballistic missiles. Republican candidate George Bush does not support either idea. The U.S. and Soviet Union agreed in Sept. 1987 to begin "full-stage negotiations," beginning with "effective verification measures which will make it possible to ratify the U.S.-U.S.S.R. threshold test ban treaty of 1974, and peaceful nuclear explosions treaty of 1976...." Joint nuclear explosions at each other's test sites to test verification measures were scheduled for the summer of 1988.

Steve Kelley, *San Diego Union*, Copley News Service.

ADMINISTRATION POLICY

The Administration wants progress in strategic arms control, but not at the price of concessions on SDI. Although Secretary of State George P. Shultz acknowledged for the first time in Mar. 1988 that agreements in both areas will probably have to be "completed more or less at the same time," no further progress has been made in breaking the deadlock. The Joint Chiefs of Staff have supported Reagan's START goals, assuming there is a continued commitment to modernize the U.S. strategic arsenal (see Chapter 3).

In regard to conventional weapons, the Administration position is that NATO must build up its conventional and chemical arsenals to balance Warsaw Pact levels before reaching agreement to reduce them. In the wake of the INF treaty, it believes such a buildup is necessary to fortify deterrence in Europe, to reassure U.S. allies of the U.S. commitment to their defense, and to give the Soviet Union an incentive to agree to significant cuts in its conventional arsenal. The Administration opposes a comprehensive test ban.

POLICY CHOICES

☐ The U.S. should agree to adhere to the narrow interpretation of the ABM treaty for 10 years in return for significant Soviet cuts in heavy land-based ICBMs.
Yes. (1) Achieving reductions in numbers of Soviet land-based ICBMs, which pose the greatest threat to U.S. security, would make it worth waiting 10 years to test a ballistic missile defense system. (2) The U.S. should not miss an arms control opportunity of this magnitude for a proposition as risky as SDI, which Dukakis has called a "technological illusion" and Jackson "a cruel hoax—one that will cost hundreds of billions of dollars."
No. (1) SDI "is our best hope to reduce the nuclear danger," according to Vice President Bush, and should not be traded away. (2) "The Democrats say we cannot afford SDI. I say we cannot afford to lag behind the Soviets in this important technology," says Bush.

☐ The U.S. should seek significant conventional reductions in Europe.
Yes. (1) The greatest military concern to NATO is the danger of a Soviet surprise attack in Europe. Reductions of Warsaw Pact conventional forces would make such an attack less likely; therefore, the U.S. should seek such an agreement. (2) The West should test Gorbachev's apparent willingness to make asymmetrical reductions.
No. (1) To counter the Warsaw Pact's numerical superiority in conventional forces, the West should give priority to building up its own forces before negotiating reductions. (2) Even asymmetrical reductions by the Soviets would be to the West's disadvantage because the West would find it far more difficult to rearm quickly than would the U.S.S.R.

☐ The U.S. should agree to a negotiated, verifi-

able ban on the flight testing of ballistic missiles.
Yes. Tests advance the development of faster and more accurate weapons, characteristics that make them suitable for first-strike weapons. They are therefore inherently destabilizing, because they raise the risk of nuclear war due to miscalculation during a crisis.

No. Weapons testing and modernization themselves do not decrease stability. On the contrary, stability in the arms race is increased if weapons are known to be accurate, reliable and survivable. Without testing, the U.S. will not know which weapons work.

SELECT BIBLIOGRAPHY

Crowe, Adm. William J., Jr., "Why the Joint Chiefs Support the INF Treaty." *Arms Control Today,* Apr. 1988, pp. 3–6. Washington, D.C., Arms Control Association, 1988. Statement to the Senate Foreign Relations Committee.

Dean, Jonathan, "Military Security in Europe." *Foreign Affairs,* Fall 1987, pp. 22–40. Argues that the U.S. should pursue force reductions in Europe.

Krepon, Michael, "Arms Control Verification and Compliance," *Headline Series* No. 270. New York, Foreign Policy Association, Sept./Oct. 1984. Overview of the difficulties.

Weinberger, Caspar W., "Arms Reductions and Deterrence." *Foreign Affairs,* Spring 1988, pp. 700–19. Former defense secretary cautions against deep reductions in the defense budget.

3

Defense: How Much Is Enough?

✔ *How much defense can the U.S. afford?*

✔ *Does the U.S. have its priorities straight?*

✔ *Should the U.S. scrap the Stealth bomber? the Trident D-5? Should it build more MX missiles?*

✔ *Is SDI deployment necessary?*

BACKGROUND

The Reagan Administration requested $299.5 billion in defense spending for fiscal year (FY) 1989. This figure, a compromise reached during the Administration-Congress "budget summit" in Nov. 1987, is $33 billion, or roughly 10%, less than the original request. In real terms (allowing for inflation), it represents a 1% drop from the FY 1988 level of $292 billion and is 10% lower than the FY 1985 peak. Support for continuing the buildup after 1985 was hurt by the growing Federal deficit, by a sense that President Ronald Reagan had achieved what he set out to do, by the resumption of arms control talks with the U.S.S.R., and by a lengthening list of scandals about waste, fraud and mismanagement among Pentagon defense contractors.

Defense budgets, after declining through most of the 1970s, increased slowly during the Carter Administration and then accelerated rapidly. During its first five years, the Reagan Administration achieved the largest peacetime military buildup in American history, at a cost of $1 trillion. Because of the general perception that U.S. military strength had declined while the Soviet Union's had grown, the Reagan buildup commanded widespread popular and congressional support.

Where the money went. During the peak years, budget authority for weapons modernization almost doubled in real terms. Funding for strategic weapons grew in real terms by 48% between FY 1981 and FY 1987. In that period, the Administration spent $227 billion on the strategic triad—land-based, sea-based and aircraft-based nuclear weapons. These included the MX and Midgetman intercontinental ballistic missiles (ICBMs), the air-launched cruise missile, the Trident submarine and its C-4 and D-5 submarine-launched ballistic missiles (SLBMs), and the B-1B and Stealth bombers.

Research also accelerated on ballistic missile defense under the Strategic Defense Initiative (SDI, popularly known as Star Wars), proposed by Reagan in 1983. Reagan saw the development of an effective shield against nuclear ballistic missile attack as preferable to a continued reliance on the fear of "mutual assured destruction" (MAD) to deter nuclear war. Work also proceeded on an antisatellite weapon (ASAT).

Funding for conventional forces rose significantly (39%) during the same period. Navy budgets increased by nearly 50% in the push to build a 600-ship fleet, including two new aircraft carrier battle groups. (The total cost for the expansion of the Navy is expected to run as high as $140 billion.) The Army and Air Force also expanded and modernized their equipment.

Pentagon reform. A sweeping overhaul of the Pentagon's management went into effect in 1986. The reform established a new under secretary of defense for acquisition, whose job is to make procurement of weapons and equipment more efficient. It also strengthened the positions of the Chairman of the Joint Chiefs of Staff and of regional commanders of U.S. forces in the field, in an attempt to lessen the impact of interservice rivalry on military efficiency.

PRIORITIES

Debate over the Administration's priorities has focused on the following issues:

Investment vs. readiness. From FY 1981 to FY 1987, funding for investment (also known as modernization—i.e. research and development, or R&D, procurement and construction) grew in real terms by 44%, while funding for readiness (support programs, including personnel, operations and maintenance, or O & M) grew by only 13%. The Administration defended this ratio on the grounds that U.S. weapons development had fallen behind. Critics charged that the U.S. was building a costly arsenal it could not afford to maintain and a "hollow" army that lacked the equipment and training to fulfill its missions. One of the largest readiness accounts is military pay, and critics fear that the Administration's success in manning the armed forces with better qualified recruits will be jeopardized in the future by Pentagon salary cuts. Readiness accounts,

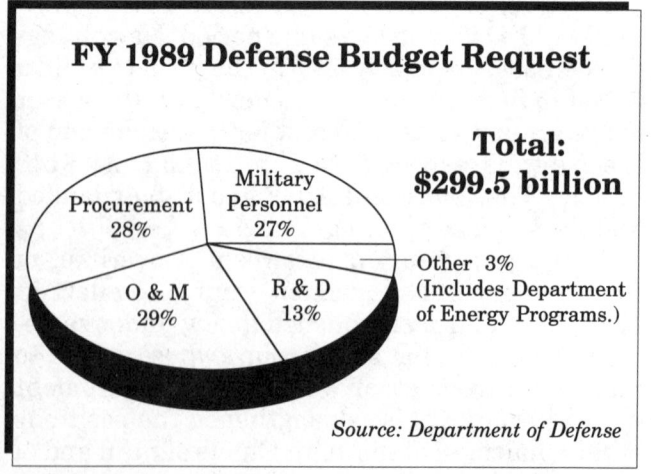

FY 1989 Defense Budget Request

Procurement 28%
Military Personnel 27%
O & M 29%
R & D 13%

Total: **$299.5 billion**

Other 3% (Includes Department of Energy Programs.)

Source: Department of Defense

they note, are always the first to be hit by budget cuts because they do not enjoy the same political protection as weapons programs.

Strategic vs. conventional weapons. Administration critics question the necessity of modernizing all three legs of the strategic triad at once and of developing two new ICBMs (MX and Midgetman) and two new bombers (the B-1B and Stealth) simultaneously. Some believe that the tremendous power and accuracy of weapons like the MX and D-5 make them so threatening to the Soviets that they add to instability and therefore decrease security. Proponents think that such improvements strengthen deterrence.

Advocates of a change in emphasis from strategic to conventional weapons gained support from a bipartisan report commissioned by the Pentagon and released in early 1988. Titled "Discriminate Deterrence," the report argues that an all-out nuclear war with the Soviet Union is increasingly unlikely and that spending so much in preparation for one detracts from the U.S. ability to meet the more likely contingency of low-level conflict elsewhere in the world. The report also notes that conventional weapons are becoming so much more accurate, powerful and cost-effective that they can now fulfill many of the same functions as nuclear weapons.

Star Wars. Reagan and his supporters think that a movement away from deterrence through fear of MAD should be a top priority. Opponents believe that a defense against nuclear weapons is too expensive. Even if it could be achieved, which they doubt, it would be destabilizing because the Soviets would develop a new generation of offensive arms to counter it.

Land vs. sea. Critics of the naval buildup believe that the Army has been shortchanged. They want the U.S. to spend more of its money bolstering its land forces, both in Europe and for use in other areas of the world, on the grounds that battles are more likely to be won or lost on land than at sea. Proponents of heavier spending

MAJOR WEAPONS PROGRAMS

	Background	Cost	Status
Strategic Defense Initiative (SDI)	Launched in 1983 to develop the technology to defend against attack by offensive nuclear ballistic missiles and ultimately to shift U.S. nuclear strategy from deterrence to defense, the program has been one of the fastest growing and most controversial items in the military budget.	For FY 1989, the Administration has asked for $5 billion, $1.7 billion less than the original 1989 proposal but about $1 billion more than Congress appropriated for 1988. Estimates of the total cost of SDI run as high as $1 trillion; the Reagan Administration now estimates about $100 billion. The program has cost $12 billion so far.	The Administration had set 1992 as a target date for deciding whether to proceed with development of a space-based missile defense system. However, it is unlikely to meet that goal given funding shortfalls in the last two years and possible delays in needed testing.
Antisatellite weapons (ASATs)	The U.S. has been working on an ASAT system since 1977; the Soviet Union already has an operational one. After the first and only U.S. ASAT test against a target in Sept. 1985, Congress blocked further testing.	ASAT development was dropped from the FY 1989 budget request, saving $750 million.	
MISSILES *MX (missile experimental)*	The MX (renamed Peacekeeper by the Reagan Administration) is a 10-warhead land-based ICBM introduced by the Carter Administration as a more accurate and powerful replacement for the aging U.S. Minuteman. Neither the Carter nor Reagan Administration was able to come up with a basing mode Congress would accept. Although it authorized funds for 50 MXs to be placed in existing Minuteman silos, Congress refused to fund 50 more until less-vulnerable bases could be found. In late 1986, the Administration decided to mount the other 50 missiles (and eventually all 100) on railcars for rapid dispersal in a crisis.	The Administration cut its request from 21 MX missiles to 12 for FY 1989, costing $809 million. It also requested $793 million to develop the rail-basing mode, $455 million less than it originally intended to ask. The program has cost $20 billion so far.	Thirty-three of the 50 MXs already funded are in place in Minuteman silos; the remaining 17 will be deployed by the end of 1988. Congress has tied funding for additional MXs to development of Midgetman, and controversy over the basing mode continues. MX has also been plagued with technical difficulties.

Midgetman (small ICBM)	The Reagan Administration decided to begin work on Midgetman, a small, single-warhead, mobile ICBM, in 1983, and began full-scale development in 1986.	All funding except for $200 million—in recognition of congressional support for the missile and in case a future Administration wants to revive it—was cut from the Midgetman program in the FY 1989 budget, saving some $2.2 million. (If completed, the program could cost nearly $40 billion.)
Trident II D-5	The most accurate undersea missile to date, the D-5, which can carry up to 10 warheads, can match the accuracy of land-based missiles.	Test flights of the D-5 have been successful; it should become operational in 1989. The Pentagon has requested $2.5 billion for 66 D-5s for FY 1989. The total cost of the program will be over $37 billion.
AIRCRAFT **B-1B bomber**	The B-1B (which was cut by Carter and restored by Reagan) was designed as an interim bomber to replace the aging B-52 until the more advanced Stealth bomber is ready in the 1990s.	Congress imposed a spending cap of $20.5 billion (in 1981 dollars, equal to $28.3 billion today) when it authorized the restoration of the program, most of which has been spent. For FY 1989, the Administration has requested $248 million for aircraft modifications. The first B-1B was delivered in July 1985; all were due to be operational by Apr. 1988. But the B-1B has been plagued by malfunctions, and experts say billions more will be needed to equip it to evade new Soviet defenses over the coming years.
Stealth (advanced technology bomber, or B-2)	Most information about the Stealth bomber, named for its ability to evade radar and infrared detection, is classified.	While not releasing exact figures, the Defense Department says Stealth will cost within 2% to 3% of the B-1B (or about $200 million to $300 million per plane). The total cost of the program is estimated to be about $39 billion. The Air Force plans to build 132 beginning in 1991.

Stayskal, 1984, *Tampa Tribune*.

on the Navy, like former Navy Secretary James H. Webb Jr., maintain that the U.S. is fundamentally a maritime nation and that the Navy, which can project American power quickly to trouble spots around the globe and guard vital sea-lanes, is the service best suited to protect U.S. interests.

ADMINISTRATION POLICY

Frank C. Carlucci's appointment as Secretary of Defense after Caspar W. Weinberger's retirement in the fall of 1987 marked the end of the Reagan Administration's attempts to block the trend toward smaller defense budgets. Carlucci made clear his intention to draw up a budget consistent with the Nov. 1987 agreement with Congress, and gave Pentagon departments two months to cut $33 billion from earlier FY 1989 budget plans. He urged the elimination of whole programs rather than stretching them out or trimming readiness accounts.

Carlucci's FY 1989 budget is the first Reagan defense request in which funding for operations and maintenance outweighs that for procure-

By Wright for the *Miami News*.

ment. It calls for cancellation of 18 entire weapons programs, including the ASAT, and a reduction of 36,000 active-duty military personnel (out of 2.1 million). The Air Force, Army and Navy are all losing men, equipment, or both, in moves the Pentagon says will save some $2.5 billion. Carlucci also called for the retirement of 16 frigates, prompting Navy Secretary Webb to resign. The cuts mean that the Navy will not reach its 600-ship goal until after 1994, instead of 1989 as planned.

Defense Department officials think that they will have to cut $200 billion from Weinberger's last five-year budget. This would allow for about 2% real annual growth, which they believe is the most that Congress will fund. Some in Congress doubt the Pentagon will even get that much.

POLICY CHOICES

❏ The U.S. should spend on defense however much is needed to protect its interests and meet its commitments.
Yes. (1) As the richest nation in the world, the U.S. can afford to pay whatever price is necessary to ensure its security. (2) The U.S. should not let

budgetary concerns dictate defense spending levels.
No. (1) Security has an economic as well as a military component. By concentrating only on military security, the U.S. is imperiling its economic security. (2) Large defense budgets do not necessarily buy greater security. Establishing budgetary limits encourages the setting of priorities and the elimination of frills.

❐ The U.S. should scrap the D-5 missile and the Stealth bomber, and should not build any more MX missiles.
Yes. (1) The functions of these weapons can be accomplished by weapons already in the U.S. strategic arsenal, which is adequate to maintain deterrence. (2) The money being spent on these systems would be better spent upgrading U.S. conventional forces and raising readiness levels.
No. (1) Canceling these programs would leave the U.S. with a dated and vulnerable mix of weapons and would weaken deterrence. (2) Scrapping these weapons would weaken the U.S. military posture and make it more difficult for the U.S. to negotiate favorable arms control agreements.

❐ The U.S. should make deploying an SDI system in the 1990s a priority.
Yes. (1) Defense-based deterrence is preferable to deterrence based on the threat of MAD. (2) Significant progress has been made in SDI research; to say that a defensive system against ballistic missiles cannot work and therefore should not be funded is a self-fulfilling prophecy. (3) The U.S. cannot afford to fall behind the Soviets in strategic defense. In Vice President George Bush's words, "I do not believe for a moment the Soviets' rhetoric that they are spending billions on a program that they do not plan to deploy."
No. (1) To be worthwhile, a defense against nuclear weapons would have to work perfectly, since even a small percentage of missiles getting through would cause unacceptable damage. Achieving such

a perfect defense is so unlikely that it should not be pursued, given the huge cost of the project. (2) Studies raise serious doubts as to whether SDI technologies—even some of the less exotic ones—would ever work reliably. (3) Pursuing SDI with the aim of deployment will not only block U.S.-Soviet efforts to reduce levels of offensive arms, but will also probably lead to a new spiral in the offensive arms race as the Soviet Union seeks to counter SDI.

SELECT BIBLIOGRAPHY

Annual Report to the Congress, Fiscal Year 1989. U.S. Department of Defense, Washington, D.C., USGPO,* Feb. 1988. Annual report on the state of the military.

Armstrong, Scott, and Grier, Peter, "Strategic Defense Initiative: Splendid Defense or Pipe Dream?" *Headline Series* No. 275. New York, Foreign Policy Association, Sept./Oct. 1985. Pros and cons of strategic defense.

"Defense and the Federal Deficit." *Great Decisions '86,* pp. 15–24. New York, Foreign Policy Association, 1986. Overview of the defense budget process and the Reagan buildup.

Defense Budget Project, Center on Budget and Policy Priorities, 236 Massachusetts Ave., N.E., Suite 301, Washington, D.C. 20002. Publishes analyses of defense spending issues.

Discriminate Deterrence: Report of the Commission on Integrated Long-Term Strategy. Washington, D.C., USGPO, 1988. Report of this bipartisan commission urges, among other things, less emphasis on nuclear weapons and more on conventional strength.

☆ ☆ ☆

* United States Government Printing Office, 710 N. Capitol Street, N.W., Washington, D.C. 20401.

4

Dealing with Terrorism

✔ *How can the U.S. combat terrorism?*
✔ *Who are the terrorists and who are their victims?*
✔ *What are the terrorists after?*

FACTS

- Over 8,000 significant incidents of international terrorism occurred between 1968 and 1986.
- An average of 10 terrorist incidents took place per day in 1986, up from 10 per week in 1976.
- As of May 1988, nine U.S. citizens were held hostage in Lebanon.

BACKGROUND

Terrorism, the systematic use of fear as a means of coercion, is a subjectively defined phenomenon. According to the cliché, one person's terrorist is another's freedom fighter. Both have political objectives and resort to violence to achieve their aims. With threats and sporadic attacks on individuals or places (an embassy, a railroad station, an army post), terrorists often communicate their messages with the media's help. Success results more from the public's fear of what terrorists might do than from actual acts of violence. Some terrorists are assassins who target individuals or groups they deem politically important. Others rely on random acts of violence to intimidate entire populations and their governments. Although skyjackings and televised interviews with hostages are relatively recent phenomena, the practice of terrorism is ancient.

International terrorism. The Russian social revolutionaries of 1905 introduced the 20th century to international terrorism: they staged attacks in Finland from headquarters in Switzerland, financed by Japanese funds laundered in the U.S. In the 1950s and early 1960s incidents of international terrorism averaged fewer than 12 per year. Most occurred in Europe and the Middle East, with a rash in Latin America following the Cuban revolution. Many European colonies adopted terrorist tactics in their struggles for independence. In the early 1960s the U.S. joined the list of terrorist targets.

The year 1968 has been called the watershed for modern terrorism. It saw the explosion of Arab terrorism following the Six-Day War of 1967, the beginnings of European terrorist movements, led by rebellious students, such as Baader-Meinhof in West Germany, and the emergence of the Provisional Irish Republican Army (IRA). The revolution in transportation and communications technology has given terrorists far greater mobility.

Today, according to U.S. Department of De-

Willis © 1985, *Dallas Times Herald*.

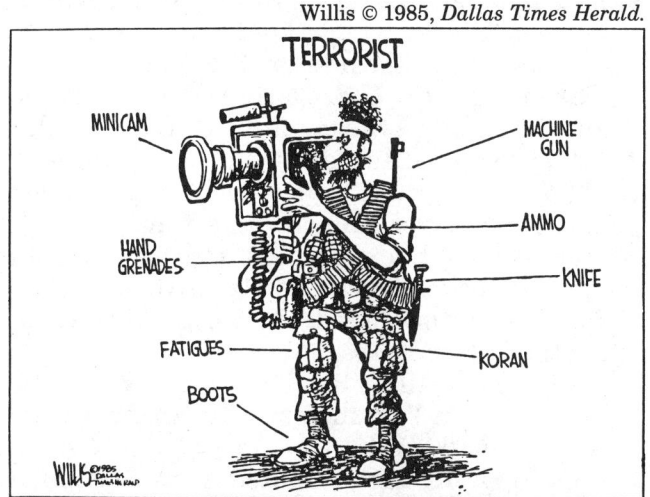

fense estimates, 40% of all terrorist incidents occur in Europe, perpetrated largely by non-Europeans; their victims, people of all nationalities. Many terrorist organizations' goals are of a peculiarly local or regional nature, often nationalist, separatist or ethnic, as with the Palestinian terrorist organizations and the Provisional IRA. Recent trends in terrorism include increasing internationalization and greater victimization of nonpolitical figures (tourists, businesspeople, etc.).

State-sponsored terrorism. Some terrorists seek state sponsors to provide them with money, arms, access to military intelligence and training in terrorist warfare. Countries most notorious for supporting international terrorism include Libya, Iran, Syria, Cuba and North Korea. A number of other countries provide sanctuaries or simply look the other way.

Superpower involvement. Both the Soviet Union and the U.S. officially condemn terrorism. However, the U.S.S.R., according to the Central Intelligence Agency (CIA), spends $200 million a year providing training and arms to international terrorist organizations, including the Palestine Liberation Organization (PLO), which passes on Soviet arms to other terrorist groups. Similarly, the U.S. has supported such antigovernment rebel groups as Renamo in Mozambique, Angola's Unita and the mujahideen in Afghanistan, organizations regarded as terrorist by the U.S.S.R.

Targeting the U.S. Early terrorist actions against the U.S. were committed by Cuban exiles who hijacked U.S. airplanes to return to Cuba in the 1960s. Americans have often been prime targets because terrorists know that the U.S., with its concern for human rights and its powerful media, will be outraged and attentive.

Major terrorist acts against U.S. citizens include the following:

• On Nov. 4, 1979, Iranian militants took the U.S. embassy in Tehran, Iran. The hostages were released Jan. 20, 1981.

• On Aug. 31, 1981, the Red Army Faction, a

successor to Baader-Meinhof, bombed U.S. Air Force headquarters in Ramstein, West Germany.
- On Oct. 23, 1983, terrorists in trucks filled with TNT attacked U.S. Marine headquarters in Beirut, Lebanon, killing 241 U.S. troops.
- On June 19, 1985, Salvadoran terrorists killed four U.S. marines and two businessmen in San Salvador, El Salvador.
- On June 30, 1985, Lebanese Shiite terrorists hijacked TWA Flight 847 and held 39 Americans hostage in Beirut for 17 days.
- From Oct. 7 to 9, 1985, four members of the Palestine Liberation Front, a faction of the PLO, held the cruise ship *Achille Lauro* hostage and killed one American.
- A bomb exploded on Apr. 5, 1986, in a discotheque in West Berlin frequented by U.S. soldiers. One U.S. citizen was killed, 60 others were injured. The U.S. blamed Libya, and on Apr. 14 the U.S. bombed two Libyan cities in retaliation.
- On Apr. 14, 1988, the Japanese Red Army, an ally of Shiite terrorists in Lebanon, was suspected of having bombed a U.S.O. club in Naples, Italy, killing five people.

The Apr. 5 to 19, 1988, hijacking of a Kuwaiti Boeing 747, apparently by the pro-Iranian Lebanese Party of God, was the most professional terrorist operation to date. The hijackers were thoroughly familiar with the aircraft and secured it against antiterrorist action.

ADMINISTRATION POLICY

U.S. policy on terrorism calls for no concessions. This policy originated in 1972 following the massacre of Israeli athletes at the Munich, West Germany, Olympics. A plethora of committees, task forces and even a special ambassador have been appointed to execute this policy. Exceptions have been made, however. The U.S. negotiated the release of the TWA Flight 847 hostages in 1985 in exchange for Palestinians held by Israel.

Also, the Administration has sometimes subordinated antiterrorist policy to other priorities. For example, Syria was omitted from the American list of states supporting terrorism after it helped obtain the release of U.S. hostages in Lebanon. In 1986 the U.S. sold arms to a country it reviled as a terrorist haven, Iran, in an effort to free hostages held in Lebanon.

Under the secret National Security Decision Directive 138 of Apr. 1984, the U.S. adopted an aggressive approach to terrorism. This policy entails holding states responsible for acts of terrorism in which their nationals are involved, undertaking preventive and retaliatory strikes against state sponsors, and improving intelligence and international cooperation.

At the May 1986 economic summit conference in Tokyo, six Western industrialized countries and Japan agreed to impose diplomatic sanctions and bar arms exports to Libya for sponsoring terrorism. The U.S. and Britain also favored economic sanctions against Libya, but Japan and Italy declined.

Finally, the Iran-contra affair (see Chapter 1) raised questions about the Administration's avowed policy on terrorism. By negotiating with Iran, a country it had called "the leading supporter of terrorism," for the release of U.S. hostages held in Lebanon, the U.S. compromised its no-concessions rule.

POLICY CHOICES

❐ The U.S. should be prepared to use military force against states that support terrorism, as it did against Libya in 1986.
Yes. (1) Terrorist attacks on the U.S. appeared to abate after the strike on Libya. (2) Making the cost of sponsoring terrorism unacceptably high will persuade states to withhold their support. (3) The only language terrorists understand is force.
No. (1) Punishment with a military strike is

Gamble © 1985, *Florida Times-Union*.

disproportionate to the crime, as well as a violation of international law. (2) Using force strains U.S. relations with its own allies. (3) Most terrorists are prepared to sacrifice their lives for their cause and no amount of force is likely to deter them.

❏ The U.S. should negotiate with terrorists under appropriate circumstances.
Yes. (1) When a U.S. citizen's life is endangered, the government should use every method available to try to save him/her. (2) Negotiation has led to the successful resolution of many previous international conflicts.
No. (1) It tells terrorists that violence pays and will encourage them to strike again. (2) Negotiating with terrorists provides them with diplomatic legitimacy.

❏ The U.S. should coordinate its response to terrorists with its allies.
Yes. An embargo or diplomatic stance taken by several countries united has a greater impact than a unilateral action.
No. The U.S. cannot afford to compromise its position on terrorism because some of its allies may disagree on a specific course of action.

SELECT BIBLIOGRAPHY

Bedlington, Stanley, *Combatting International Terrorism: U.S.-Allied Cooperation and Political Will.* Washington, D.C., The Atlantic Council of the U.S. (1616 H St., N.W., Washington, DC 20006), Nov. 1986. Policy paper prepared for nonpartisan Atlantic council's project on terrorism.

Gutteridge, William, ed., *Contemporary Terrorism.* New York, Facts on File for the Institute for the Study of Conflict, 1986. Includes four case studies.

Laqueur, Walter, *The Age of Terrorism.* Boston, Mass., Little, Brown, 1987. Updated classic analyzes terrorism, using historical examples.

Whitehead, John C., "Terrorism: The Challenge and the Response." *Department of State Bulletin,* Feb. 1987, pp. 70–73. Address by deputy secretary of state.

5

Trade, the Dollar and Foreign Investment

✔ *How can the U.S. boost exports?*
✔ *Should the U.S. try to arrest the dollar's fall?*
✔ *Is foreign investment in the U.S. good for the country?*

FACTS

- The U.S. is the world's largest economy, the largest consumer market, the largest importer and second largest exporter—after West Germany. With less than 5% of the world's population, the U.S. produces 22% of the world's industrial goods.
- In 1987, some 70% of U.S. manufactured products had to compete with a foreign product, as compared with 25% in 1960. Of the goods manufactured in the U.S., 88% require imported parts and materials.
- In 1987, the U.S. trade deficit reached a record $171 billion.
- The U.S. became the world's largest debtor nation in 1985.

The deficit in the U.S. balance of payments (the record of all economic transactions between the U.S. and the rest of the world in a given period, usually one year) is a sign that more money is flowing out of the U.S. than in and constitutes a drain on the country's future resources. Possible repercussions include job losses in industries that are not competitive or face unfair foreign competition; a lowered standard of living as the U.S. sends billions of dollars in interest payments abroad; and strains in U.S. alliances with more-successful trading nations, particularly Japan. Policy options range from closing off trade by protectionism to doing nothing, with probably a majority of Americans favoring a trade policy somewhere in between, one that would cover their contradictory goals: to preserve U.S. jobs, keep the economy growing and cut the trade deficit—and still be able to buy inexpensive imported TVs, tape recorders, cars and other foreign products.

BACKGROUND

Great Depression. High tariffs caused world trade to contract and helped push the U.S. into the Great Depression of the 1930s. Since then the U.S. has advocated free trade as a path to economic growth and political stability. According to free-traders, if each country trades those things it makes relatively more cheaply than others (known as comparative advantage) and trade barriers are low, world trade and world income will expand.

The gold standard and GATT. As World War II came to a close, the U.S. and its allies laid the foundation for a new free-trading order. The **Bretton Woods** conference of 1944 established the rules by which the exchange rates between currencies were determined. The price of gold was fixed at $35 an ounce and all other countries set the value of their currency in terms of the dollar. It was hoped this new "gold standard" would bring about a more stable international economy.

The U.S. also led its allies in the formation of the General Agreement on Tariffs and Trade (GATT) in 1947. The key to GATT is **"most-favored-nation" treatment:** if one GATT member gives a trade advantage to another, it

"HOWDY! DID I HEAR A CALL FOR HELP?..."

By H. Payne for Scripps Howard.

should give the same advantage to every other GATT member. In this way, all members trade on an equal footing. Membership in GATT has grown from the original 23 countries to 96 in 1988. In the course of seven rounds of negotiations, tariffs were reduced from an average of 40% to less than 5% today.

Is freer trade still in the U.S. interest? This question was raised in the 1970s when the U.S. seemed to lose its competitive edge in traditionally profitable, high-employment industries: automobiles, steel and textiles. The U.S. ability to compete was hurt by inflation, high energy costs, old equipment and high wages. In 1971 the U.S. had a deficit in its merchandise trade balance (the difference in the value of goods imported and goods exported) for the first time since the late 19th century. In moves it hoped would reduce the pressure against the overvalued dollar and the trade deficit, the Nixon Administration suspended the convertibility of the dollar into gold and imposed a 10% surcharge on U.S. imports. Since that time the dollar has "floated" in value: the greater the demand for dollars (whether because the U.S. economy is growing, interest on U.S. securities is high, or American goods are sought), the greater the dollar's value.

Reaganomics. By Apr. 1988, the U.S. was in

its 65th straight month of economic expansion; the rate of growth of the gross national product (GNP), adjusted for inflation, had averaged 2.8% (1981–86); in 1987 the rate was 2.9%. At the same time, unemployment fell from a high of 9.7% in 1982 to 5.4% by Apr. 1988. Inflation in 1987 was 4.4%. But critics charge that these solid achievements are undermined by the other legacies of the Ronald Reagan years: a Federal debt of $2.4 trillion as of 1987, up from $74 billion in 1981, a record trade deficit, and increasing purchases of U.S. assets by foreign investors. Like a household that runs up large bills, the U.S. will have to service its record debt for years to come.

In 1987 the U.S. had a trade deficit of $171 billion. The largest portion by far was in merchan-

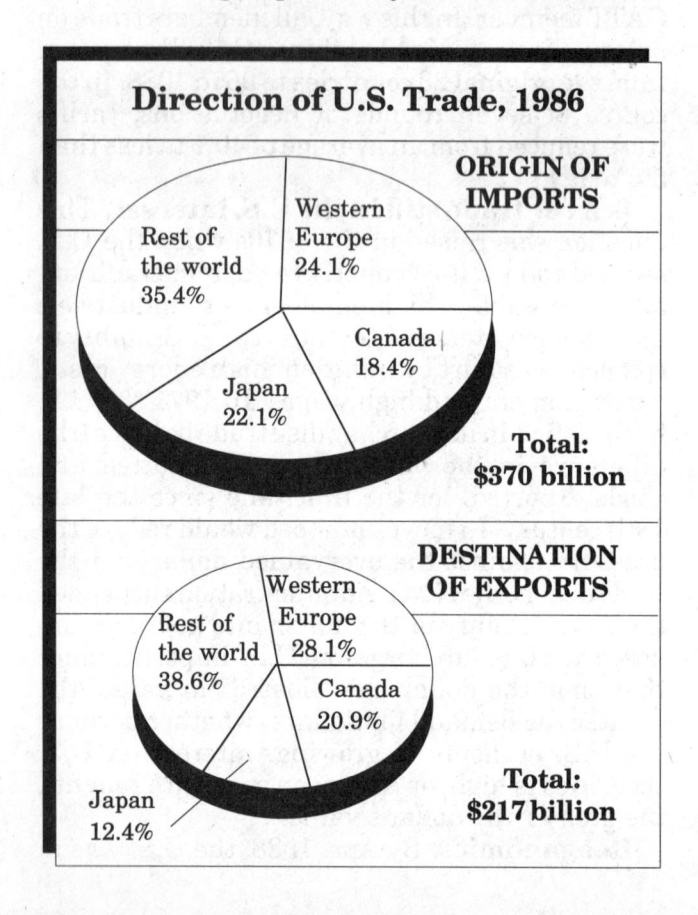

Direction of U.S. Trade, 1986

ORIGIN OF IMPORTS
- Rest of the world 35.4%
- Western Europe 24.1%
- Canada 18.4%
- Japan 22.1%

Total: $370 billion

DESTINATION OF EXPORTS
- Rest of the world 38.6%
- Western Europe 28.1%
- Canada 20.9%
- Japan 12.4%

Total: $217 billion

dise trade, which was offset somewhat by a surplus in services. Even merchandise trade had some bright spots. Agricultural exports increased for the second year in a row and were expected to continue climbing in 1988. Exports of manufactures also rose.

Among the culprits blamed for the U.S. trade deficit are record Federal budget deficits; a decline in the quality of U.S. goods; multinational corporations (MNCs) that have moved their factories overseas and whose sales to the U.S. are counted as imports; slow economic growth in major foreign markets; and unfair trade practices by U.S. trading partners.

THE DOLLAR

The overvalued dollar of the 1980s hurt exports; in effect, it acted like a tax on U.S. producers and a subsidy for foreign producers. Although initially pleased at the dollar's strength as a sign of foreign faith in the U.S. economy, the Administration had changed its mind by 1985 as the trade situation deteriorated. In Sept. 1985, Treasury Secretary James A. Baker 3d and Federal Reserve Chairman Paul Volcker held a meeting at the Plaza Hotel in New York City with finance ministers from Britain, France, Japan and West Germany (known as the Group of 5). The group's statement that "further orderly appreciation of the main nondollar currencies against the dollar is desirable" gave momentum to a drop in the dollar that had begun some months before.

Since 1985 the dollar has fallen sharply, having dropped to 50% of its value against the Japanese yen and the West German mark by the fall of 1987. Following the Oct. 1987 stock market crash, the Reagan Administration stepped in to prop up the dollar. In Dec. 1987 and Apr. 1988, the Group of 7 (the Group of 5 plus Canada and Italy) pledged to keep the dollar from falling further.

FOREIGN INVESTMENT

Foreign investors, attracted by the low price of U.S. properties, have been buying U.S. assets. There are two types of foreign investment: **foreign direct investment** (the acquisition or purchase of an asset, such as a factory or land) and **portfolio investment** (the purchase of stocks, bonds and government securities). Most of the foreign money is in securities because interest rates in the last few years have been high. Except for certain industries defined as strategic, there are now no restrictions on foreign investment.

Advocates of foreign investment argue that it has helped bridge the gap between Federal spending and American savings that accounts for the budget deficit. Without this money, interest rates and taxes would have had to be raised. Furthermore, foreign investment has created or preserved over 2.5 million jobs. All told, foreign investors own a very small part of the U.S. economy.

Still, foreign investment worries some Americans. An editorial in *Forbes* in Jan. 1988 cautioned that "by using just last year's trade surplus with the U.S. of $60 billion, Japan could buy enough stock in a half-dozen of our biggest companies . . . to in effect control 'em."

ADMINISTRATION POLICY

"We remain as opposed as ever to protectionism because America's growth and future depend on trade" (Reagan, 1987). Reagan has remained committed to free trade throughout his presidency, though he has been forced on occasion to make a strategic retreat (e.g., pressuring Japan beginning in 1981 for so-called voluntary export quotas on its cars, and placing higher tariffs and import quotas on specialty steels in 1983). Reagan took two major steps to open up trade. (1) He supported a new round of GATT negotiations for

By Wasserman for *The Boston Globe*.

which the groundwork was laid at Punta del Este, Uruguay, in Sept. 1986. The agenda includes trade in services, agricultural subsidies and other nontariff barriers. (2) In Oct. 1987, the U.S. reached an accord with Canada, its largest trading partner, on a comprehensive trade pact (see Chapter 14). It negotiated a less comprehensive agreement with Mexico in Nov. 1987 (see Chapter 15).

The omnibus trade bill, the most comprehensive trade legislation produced since 1974, was passed overwhelmingly by the House in Apr. 1988 but in the Senate by a majority too small to override a presidential veto. The bill contained features favored by the Administration, including authority to negotiate the Uruguay Round of GATT; a new system of harmonized tariffs; and stronger laws protecting U.S. patented intellectual property. But the President objected to the bill's requirement that plants with more than 100 workers give a 60-day notice before a closing or long-term layoff. The Administration was also not entirely happy with a provision requiring retaliation against proven unfair trade practices, even though the bill provided several escape clauses. In May the President vetoed the bill.

The Reagan Administration has made no amendments to the long-standing U.S. policy of not restricting foreign investment in this country. Said Reagan of foreign investment in 1983: "We believe there are only winners, no losers, and all participants gain from it."

POLICY CHOICES

❐ Congress should require the President to retaliate against countries that unfairly restrict U.S. exports.
Yes. (1) The U.S. cannot succeed as a trader if it is playing by a different—less restrictive—set of rules from other countries. (2) By forcing other countries to trade fairly, the U.S. would actually be encouraging trade, since it would be forcing the increase of exports.
No. (1) The U.S. itself restricts some 18% of its imports. If the U.S. puts conditions on other countries' trade, they may begin to do the same to the U.S. (2) Congress, by mandating that the President retaliate against unfair trade practices, reduces his flexibility. The amount of U.S. trade lost because of unfair trading practices is very small.

❐ The U.S. should negotiate with major trading partners to reduce currency fluctuations and improve economic stability.
Yes. If the dollar were more stable, the U.S. and other countries would not suffer from the sudden swings in value of their currencies; this more stable environment would encourage trade.
No. Since negotiations are unlikely to produce results satisfactory to the U.S., the U.S. should avoid them.

❐ The U.S. should restrict foreign direct investment.
Yes. (1) Foreign direct investment threatens the sovereignty of the U.S., leaving it potentially de-

pendent on decisions by foreign countries. (2) At a minimum, the U.S. should increase reporting requirements so that it knows precisely how much property is owned by foreigners.

No. (1) The benefits of foreign investment, particularly the jobs created, more than outweigh any potential threat. (2) Reporting requirements are already strict and increasing them will only scare off foreign investors.

SELECT BIBLIOGRAPHY

"Foreign Investment in the U.S.: The Selling of America?" *Great Decisions 1987,* pp. 55–64. New York, Foreign Policy Association, 1987. Introduction to foreign investment.

Tolchin, Martin, and Tolchin, Susan, "Foreign Money, U.S. Fears." *The New York Times Magazine,* Dec. 13, 1987, pp. 63–68. Examines the major sources of foreign investment in the U.S.

"U.S. Trade and Global Markets: Risks and Opportunities." *Great Decisions 1988*, pp. 25–36. New York, Foreign Policy Association, 1988. Overview of U.S. trade position.

Yeutter, Clayton, "U.S. Trade Policy and the Trade Deficit." *Department of State Bulletin,* Apr. 1987, pp. 22–30. An appendix contains "The President's Trade Policy: An Update." Report of the U.S. trade representative.

6

Foreign Aid and the Third World

✔ *Does the U.S. provide enough foreign aid?*
✔ *What is the proper mix between military and economic aid?*
✔ *Should the U.S. channel more funds through the World Bank?*

North and South compared:	Less-developed countries	Developed countries	World
Number of countries	144	32	176
Population (billions, mid-1987)	3.86	1.16	5.02
Population growth rate (annual)	2.1%	0.6%	1.7%
Per capita GNP ($U.S., 1985)	$720	$10,169	$2,899
Per capita real GNP growth rate (average annual, 1965–85)	2.7%	1.7%	2.5%
Exports f.o.b. ($U.S., 1986)	$0.48 trillion	$1.65 trillion	$2.14 trillion
Imports c.i.f. ($U.S., 1986)	$0.50 trillion	$1.72 trillion	$2.22 trillion
Source: *Growth, Exports, & Jobs in a Changing World Economy: Agenda 1988.*			

BACKGROUND

Less-developed countries (LDCs) are sometimes referred to, collectively, as the Third World, or the South, in contrast to the developed countries (DCs) of the industrialized North. The diverse regions that comprise the Third World contain 77% of the world's population and generate 19% of the gross world product.

At one end of the LDC spectrum are the 42 poorest countries, with per capita annual incomes of $400 or less. These include 29 African countries, 12 Asian, and one Caribbean (Haiti). They produce mainly primary commodities and are heavily dependent on outside aid. At the other end are the newly industrializing countries, or NICs, of East Asia and Latin America.

The U.S. and the Third World. From 1950 to 1980, the LDCs as a whole achieved a high rate of economic growth. In the 1970s they emerged as important participants in the international economy, and U.S. trade with them grew at the rate of 6% a year. By 1981 the Third World bought more U.S. manufactured and agricultural exports than Japan and Western Europe combined. The Third World in turn provided the U.S. with vital raw materials (including 90%–100% of its manganese, bauxite and cobalt); traditional labor-intensive products such as clothing, textiles and shoes; and, to an increasing extent, electrical machinery, chemicals and transport equipment.

The global economic recession of the early 1980s, brought on by the oil price hikes of 1978–79 and tight credit policies in the U.S., had a devastating effect on both North and South. As growth rates in the industrialized countries fell and interest rates soared, demand for LDC goods declined and growth came to a halt. Whereas 40% of total U.S. trade in 1981 had been with the Third World, by 1986 it had fallen to 34%. The decline in foreign exchange earnings hurt, among others, the middle-income countries, notably Mexico,

Brazil and Argentina, whose rapid expansion in the 1970s was fueled in large measure by loans. They now found themselves hard put to meet their debt-service payments to commercial banks. The continuing debt crisis remains a major obstacle to Third World growth and development.

Development. Development means at a minimum alleviating poverty and human suffering—hunger, disease, illiteracy. Industrialized countries that have the means to aid LDCs often have different goals from theirs. The U.S. ranks democracy and human rights high on its list of development goals. India and China emphasize economic self-sufficiency; Iran and Saudi Arabia, religion-based government; Tanzania, social and economic equality.

Disagreements abound not only on goals but on the obstacles to development and the strategies to overcome them. Aid-givers, like the International Bank for Reconstruction and Development, or World Bank, and the U.S., often impose conditions on aid that LDCs find objectionable. Many LDCs, while demanding free access to DCs' markets, keep their own economies closed to protect industries and promote exports.

The World Bank is the largest single source of development funds. It makes loans for specific long-term projects and also helps countries meet short-term problems. The poorest LDCs can borrow from the World Bank's affiliate, the International Development Association (IDA), which makes loans for longer terms at lower interest rates.

Population trends. Although LDC birthrates have declined steadily over the past 20 years, so too have death rates, and consequently population growth rates remain high, outstripping economic growth and swelling the ranks of the unemployed. Furthermore, an increasing number of women are reaching childbearing age, a figure that could double by the year 2000.

The highest population growth (2.9%) is occurring in that area of the world least able to support it, sub-Saharan Africa, where per capita real income has declined since 1965 and where women bear an average of six to eight children. Rapid population growth obliges governments to divert scarce funds from development to basic human needs. It also places stress on the environment, strains social and political institutions, and increases the potential for political instability.

A birthrate of about 2.1%, the level at which births and deaths are balanced, is considered conducive to progress in development. Only four LDCs have reached this level—the same countries that have achieved rapid and successful industrial growth: Hong Kong, Singapore, South Korea and Taiwan.

Curbing population growth. Today, most governments consider family planning an essential complement to their development efforts, although many have been slow to allocate the necessary resources. Governmental sanction of family planning can help make the concept more acceptable to a country's population: in sub-Saharan Africa, 13 governments have now issued official population policies. Development policies that expand economic opportunities, increase social services, raise literacy rates and improve the status of women also contribute indirectly to lowering fertility rates. Even in countries where economic development lags, family planning and increased use of contraceptives have reduced the fertility rate.

China has relied on government incentives (pay increases, housing, better education) as well as coercive disincentives (fines and criticism) to promote its controversial "one-child" family policy. China reduced the fertility rate from 5.5% in 1960 to 2.4% in 1987.

Food. Sub-Saharan Africa, which was self-sufficient in food in the 1960s, suffered a famine in 1984 that threatened the lives of 150 million people. A continent-wide drought (1981–83) was only the most immediate cause: Africa's inability to feed itself derives from a combination of rapid population growth, widespread soil erosion and desertification, political instability, flawed development policies and an inadequate transportation system. Like many LDCs, most African countries have devoted their arable land to growing cash crops for export rather than grain crops for domestic consumption. African governments further discourage food production by imposing price controls and assigning a lower priority to agriculture than to industry. The cost of importing the grain needed to feed the continent—some 20% of African food needs by 1984—rose 600% between 1970 and 1980, while the prices of commodities exported by African nations fell. When the drought hit, countries found themselves with neither food nor the export revenues to buy it. Massive food aid, then as now, alleviated short-term suffering, but also tended to discourage agricultural production by increasing supplies and lowering prices.

U.S. aid policy. The large-scale use of aid, both economic and military, as a foreign policy instrument began after World War II. Until the early 1950s, most American aid went to Western Europe under the Marshall Plan; thereafter it went increasingly to the Third World. The U.S. today provides foreign aid to promote peace in the Middle East (primarily to Israel and Egypt), to help secure base rights for U.S. forces overseas (for example, in Turkey and the Philippines), to counter Soviet influence in Southwest Asia and Central America, and to promote development programs that support U.S. economic and humanitarian objectives.

The U.S. provides three kinds of aid to the Third World: **security assistance** (which includes all military assistance programs and economic support funds) for countries of strategic importance to the U.S.; **development assistance** for long-term economic growth and political stability; and **humanitarian assistance** for disaster relief. The primary channel for bilateral development and humanitarian aid is the Agency for

U.S. Foreign Aid Appropriations, FY 1988	
Bilateral development, humanitarian, other	$ 2.89 billion
Multilateral	$ 1.45 billion
Security: Economic Support Fund (ESF) Military	$ 3.20 billion $ 5.37 billion
Food Aid	$ 1.06 billion
Total	$13.97 billion

International Development (AID) which provides loans and grants. Security assistance is provided by the State and Defense departments. The U.S. also contributes to development through multilateral organizations such as the World Bank, the International Monetary Fund (IMF) and the United Nations Development Program (UNDP). The U.S. relies more on bilateral than multilateral aid channels because doing so gives it greater control over the disposition of funds.

Military assistance and ESF. U.S. foreign aid grew from $9.6 billion in 1980 to a peak of $20.2 billion in 1985. All of the increase went to military and economic security assistance; development aid actually declined. In 1987, total foreign aid (excluding food) dropped to $12.9 billion, of which $8.6 billion was for security assistance. Two countries, Israel and Egypt, received 39% of the total foreign aid budget. Another 10% went to "base rights" countries—Greece, the Philippines, Portugal, Spain and Turkey.

Economic support funds, which totaled $3.6 billion in 1987, are classified as economic assistance. But Administration critics think they should be classified as military aid since they only go to countries of strategic importance to the U.S., 90% of which have middle- or high-level incomes, and enable them to spend more of their own money for military purposes.

ADMINISTRATION POLICY

The Administration's approach to development emphasizes "market forces as the key to economic development." Through its trade and aid programs, the U.S. seeks to support policies that encourage a lessening of state intervention in Third World economies and promote private enterprise, the development of competitive markets, the expansion of trade, and increased private investment in Third World economies. The U.S. contributes to the World Bank and other international financial institutions. Under the 1985 Baker Plan, initiated by U.S. Treasury Secretary James A. Baker 3d, the U.S. has sought to encourage additional lending by American commercial banks to the 17 most heavily indebted Third World countries, provided they adopt free market-oriented economic policies. It has been critical of the banks' response. The World Bank estimated in 1988 that private lending would have to triple over three years to resolve the debt crisis.

In its trade policy, the U.S. tries to maintain "as open a market as possible," although it admits that there are substantial barriers to some exports critical to the Third World (sugar and textiles, for example). The U.S. participates, along with other DCs, in the Generalized System of Preferences (GSP) which gives LDCs preferred access to DC markets.

In its population policy, the U.S. has reduced funding for international family planning programs by 20% since 1985 and has significantly changed its approach. Funding now goes only to programs that provide freedom of choice in family planning and do not "perform or actively promote abortion." The U.S. no longer contributes to the UN Fund for Population Activities because of grants made to China, which AID has accused of pursuing a family planning program based on "abortion and coercion" (China has denied the charge). It has also cut off funding to the International Planned Parenthood Federation because of the organization's support of family planning that includes abortion.

The U.S. Department of Agriculture's Food for Peace program provides surplus U.S. grain and other agricultural commodities to food-short LDCs.

POLICY CHOICES

❐ The U.S. should continue to reduce aid to less-developed countries.
Yes. (1) In an era of budget cuts, the U.S. must concentrate on pressing domestic needs. (2) Past aid has often failed to make countries self-supporting. (3) Much aid is wasted, abused or misused.
No. (1) The U.S., the world's richest nation, ranks last among the 18 major aid donors (measured as a percentage of GNP) and is not discharging its moral responsibility to help the world's poorest. (2) Aid is in the U.S. interest; it is not a giveaway since 70% of bilateral aid is spent in the U.S. (3) Providing development aid is the most cost-effective way for the U.S. to protect its interests without direct involvement.

❐ The U.S. should spend more on development assistance, less on military aid and ESF.
Yes. (1) Instability in the Third World arising from economic and social inequities is a greater threat to U.S. security today than the military threats the U.S. has focused on in the past. (2) The economic well-being of the U.S. is closely linked to that of the Third World, as the debt crisis and large U.S. trade deficits of the 1980s have demonstrated.
No. (1) The U.S. is already devoting a substantial proportion of aid to development. (2) Further reductions in military assistance would compromise U.S. interests in critical areas such as the

Middle East and would cost the U.S. significant leverage.

❒ The U.S. should channel a larger proportion of aid through multilateral institutions.
Yes. (1) Because of the World Bank's burden-sharing provisions, one dollar of U.S. aid allotted to the bank permits it to lend $60. (2) Multilateral aid is oriented toward long-term development; bilateral aid is frequently used to fulfill a donor's short-term political objectives.
No. (1) Bilateral aid is frequently more efficient and effective. (2) Bilateral aid gives the U.S. greater control over the disposition of its funds.

SELECT BIBLIOGRAPHY

Armacost, Michael H., "U.S. Policy Toward the Third World." *Department of State Bulletin,* Jan. 1987, pp. 56–60. Administration policy.

Eberstadt, Nick, "Famine, Development & Foreign Aid." *Commentary,* Mar. 1985, pp. 25–31. Argues against foreign aid.

Sewell, John W., and Tucker, Stuart K., *Growth, Exports, & Jobs in a Changing World Economy: Agenda 1988.* New Brunswick, N.J., Transaction Books, 1988. Overseas Development Council study includes valuable statistical annexes.

"Third World Development: Old Problems, New Strategies?" *Great Decisions '86,* pp. 55–64. New York, Foreign Policy Association, 1986. Overview.

Walker, Brian W., "Authentic Development in Africa." *Headline Series* No. 274. New York, Foreign Policy Association, May/June 1985. Study of African problems and recommendations.

7

International Drug Traffic

✔ *Should the U.S. military play a greater role in preventing illegal drugs from entering this country?*

✔ *Should the U.S. give priority to curbing demand rather than cutting off the supply of drugs?*

✔ *Should any currently illicit drugs be legalized?*

BACKGROUND

Drug abuse has been an international problem since the last century, when the use of opium in China became widespread. The U.S. has been involved in trying to stop the drug trade since around 1900. Cocaine and heroin have been restricted by Federal regulations since 1914; marijuana since 1937. Whereas only about 2% of Americans had ever tried an illegal drug at the beginning of the 1960s, by 1985 close to 40%—some 70 million people—had done so. Today, an estimated 80% of young people have tried drugs by their mid-20s. With an estimated 1.2 million addicts and some 23 million recreational users, the U.S. is the world's largest market for illegal drugs.

Coca leaf, from which cocaine is made, comes chiefly from Peru, Bolivia, Colombia and Ecuador and is converted to cocaine primarily in Colombian laboratories. Marijuana is grown mainly in

Mexico, Colombia, Jamaica and Belize; and opium poppies used in making heroin are grown primarily in Burma, Afghanistan, Iran, Laos, Pakistan, Mexico and Thailand. Governments in these supplier nations exercise less than effective control over their territory, and corruption is widespread. The production, refining, trafficking and use of illegal drugs in these countries follow a basic pattern: opium poppy and coca leaf cultivators are typically poor farmers who live in isolated rural and often mountainous areas. Their own use of the drugs is usually socially acceptable and may be widespread. For many producers, opium and coca are their only cash crops.

Big business. The international drug trade is worth roughly $47 billion annually. According to the U.S. State Department, Mexico is "the largest single-country source of the heroin available in the U.S.," and serves as a transit point for one third of the cocaine that enters this country. Lately, however, Mexican drug dealers are being outstripped in wealth and power by the Medellín cocaine cartel, named after Colombia's second largest city. Although the cartel numbers only a handful of men, it is the source of 80% of the world's cocaine and earns profits of some $3 billion a year. Through a campaign of assassination and intimidation, the cartel has come to wield enormous political influence in Colombia and other Latin American countries.

The enormous profitability of the cocaine trade is another factor behind the cartel's clout: it earned Colombia some $1–$2 billion in foreign exchange in 1987, or about as much as Colombian coffee exports. The cartel recently offered to pay off Colombia's $10 billion foreign debt if the government would cancel its extradition treaty with the U.S., under which many of the drug lords could be tried in this country for murder and racketeering.

Colombia is not the only Latin American country where drugs are king. In Feb. 1988, Panamanian leader Gen. Manuel Antonio Noriega was indicted in Florida on charges of drug trafficking and permitting the laundering of drug profits through Panamanian banks. Witnesses testified at Senate Foreign Relations subcommittee hearings on Panama and the drug trade that Noriega's drug dealing had involved almost every institution in the country. The hearings also leveled charges at the government of Prime Minister Lynden O. Pindling of the Bahamas, a favorite transit point for drug traffickers. Other havens are Costa Rica, Honduras and Haiti.

Despite growing international cooperation and efforts by individual countries to curb the drug trade, the State Department in 1988 reported that production of coca, marijuana and opium poppy crops had grown sharply in the previous year. World production of cocaine has increased 10 times as fast as production of other illegal drugs, and the State Department predicts that coca production will continue to grow between 5% and 10% annually unless an effective herbicide which can be sprayed on fields to eradicate the coca plant is developed.

The legalization debate. The failure of drug enforcement measures to halt or even slow the flow of illegal drugs into this country has prompted some to question whether the present approach does not cause greater harm to society than do the drugs themselves. Those who argue for legalization of drugs say that it would drive down prices, put drug cartels out of business and halt the violence that is their trademark. It would also, they say, reduce drug-related crime in this country, thereby reducing pressure on U.S. law enforcement agencies, courts and prisons, and would save the government billions of dollars. Opponents counter that wider availability of purer, cheaper drugs would lead to an increase in the number of addicts and to a rise in the serious health and social problems associated with drug use. They also point out that few who favor legalization have given much thought to the vast bureaucratic difficulties that government regulation of drug sales would entail.

ADMINISTRATION POLICY

The Reagan Administration has more than tripled its spending on drug law enforcement over the last seven years—from $800 million in fiscal year (FY) 1981 to $2.5 billion in FY 1988. Over three quarters of the $21 billion the Administration has spent on fighting the illegal drug trade has gone toward crop eradication programs in drug-producing countries and antismuggling operations offshore and at the U.S.-Mexican border. The Drug Enforcement Administration (DEA), in cooperation with local police, has also seized millions of dollars worth of assets bought with drug profits. Despite record numbers of arrests and drug confiscations, U.S. consumption of cocaine and crack (a cheap and potent form of cocaine) has more than doubled since 1982, heroin consumption is on the rise, and the incidence of drug-related violence in major U.S. cities has risen substantially. In an attempt to cut down casual drug use, the Administration in 1988 adopted a "zero tolerance" policy. If the U.S. Customs Service finds as much as a trace of drugs in a car or on a ship, it can seize the vehicle. Funding for drug-abuse prevention and treatment programs for FY 1988 is $940 million.

Under the 1986 Anti-Drug Abuse Act (passed in the aftermath of basketball star Len Bias' death due to a cocaine overdose), the U.S. must annually certify that 25 countries listed by the State Department as major sources of illegal drugs are "cooperating fully" with the U.S. to stop the flow. If they lose their certification, these countries stand to lose half their U.S. aid and other benefits. But the Administration has been reluctant to penalize some U.S. allies that are known drug sources because of conflicting "national interests." For example, despite DEA objections, President Ronald Reagan once again certified Mexico in early 1988 and, until that year, had repeatedly certified Panama, despite U.S. knowledge of Noriega's involvement in drug trafficking and money laundering. Laos, an increasingly important producer of heroin, has been certified largely because the U.S. still hopes to account for some 500 Americans missing in that country since the Vietnam War.

Budget cuts have hurt some of the agencies charged with drug enforcement. The Coast Guard, for example, had its 1988 budget cut by $100 million and estimates that it will have to reduce patrols this year by 55% as a result.

Military involvement. The Defense Department has generally resisted attempts to enlist U.S. military forces in the war against drugs, partly because of a traditional bias against using the military for civilian law enforcement. Although the armed forces spent $389 million in 1987 interdicting drug traffic, studies show they had little impact on the long-term availability of drugs in the U.S. In May 1988 both houses of Congress passed a military funding bill giving Defense a wider drug role.

POLICY CHOICES

❐ The U.S. should focus on limiting demand rather than reducing the supply of illegal drugs.

Yes. (1) Efforts to reduce the supply of drugs have failed. There is a need for more treatment and education to halt the use of drugs and stiffer penalties for users and dealers. (2) Where efforts to cut off drug supplies have succeeded, prices have risen, making the drug trade even more profitable, and there has been an increase in drug-related crime. (3) Placing the blame for U.S. drug consumption on drug-producing countries has created an anti-American backlash.

No. (1) Increased funding for interdiction efforts has resulted in greater numbers of arrests and confiscations. (2) The U.S. should first make a serious commitment to reducing the drug supply—which it has not yet done. (3) It would be impossible to enforce drug laws that target users when there are so many.

❏ The U.S. military should take on a greater role in interdicting the flow of drugs into this country.
Yes. This is a national security issue, and the military is in the best position to provide personnel and equipment in the war against drugs.
No. Law enforcement is a civilian, not a military, function. Assigning the military to drug interdiction will drain money and personnel from essential military programs.

❏ The U.S. should legalize marijuana, cocaine and other illicit drugs.
Yes. Legalization would drive down the price of these drugs, making it less profitable to be in the business, and would reduce levels of drug-related violence here and abroad.
No. Legalization would lead to a major increase in numbers of drug users, bringing with it large increases in numbers of addicts and serious associated health and social problems.

SELECT BIBLIOGRAPHY

Kerr, Peter, "The Unspeakable Is Debated: Should Drugs Be Legalized?" *The New York Times,* May 15, 1988, p. A1. Pros and cons.

Nadelman, Ethan A., "U.S. Drug Policy: A Bad Export." *Foreign Policy,* Spring 1988, pp. 83–108. Argues enforcement measures cause more problems than the drug trade itself.

Shultz, George P., "Narcotics: A Global Threat." *Department of State Bulletin,* Aug. 1987, pp. 45–46. Address by the Secretary of State, May 4, 1987.

"The Traffic in Drugs: America's Global War." *The New York Times,* Apr. 10–12, 1988. Three-part series.

8

Central America

- ✔ **Will the Reagan Doctrine prevail in Central America?**
- ✔ **What are the chances for stability in the region?**
- ✔ **What are U.S. interests in Central America?**

The countries compared:	Population (millions) mid-1988 (est.)	Per capita GNP ($U.S.) 1986	External debt ($U.S., billions)
Costa Rica	2.9	$1,420	$4.2
El Salvador	5.4	$820	$1.7
Guatemala	8.7	$930	$2.6
Honduras	4.8	$740	$2.7
Nicaragua	3.6	$790	$5.6
Panama	2.3	$2,330	n.a.

Sources: *1988 World Population Data Sheet* and *World Development Report 1987*.

BACKGROUND

Central America, colonized by the Spanish in the beginning of the 16th century, declared its independence in 1821, succumbed to civil war, and by 1839 was divided into the present five countries of El Salvador, Nicaragua, Guatemala,

Honduras and Costa Rica. A sixth, Panama, did not achieve independence from Colombia until 1903. (Belize, a former British colony in Central America, is considered part of the Caribbean community of nations.)

Central America's economies are largely dependent on export crops (coffee, sugar, bananas), making them vulnerable to sharp swings in commodity prices. Commodity price decreases and oil price increases in the 1970s, together with the global economic recession of the early 1980s, hurt the region's economic growth. Central America also suffers from inequitable land and income distribution and a history of repressive dictators and the rebels who fight them. Closely tied to the U.S. economy, Central Americans admire U.S. stability and prosperity but also feel that the U.S. does not respect their sovereignty. They resent past U.S. support of unpopular dictatorships (like that of the Somoza family in Nicaragua) and are disappointed with U.S. economic leadership, especially on debt matters.

In 1978–79, political upheaval and civil war erupted in two Central American nations, El Salvador and Nicaragua, plunging the region into turmoil. The U.S. has backed the government in El Salvador and the contras, anti-Sandinista government rebels, in Nicaragua; the Soviet Union and Cuba have supported the rebels in El Salvador and the Nicaraguan government. In 1982 Mexico, Panama, Venezuela and Colombia formed the Contadora Group in an attempt to restore stability in the area. Their efforts paved the way for the Aug. 1987 peace initiative of Costa Rican President Oscar Arias Sánchez, which won him the Nobel Peace Prize. The peace agreement (the Guatemala accord), signed by the presidents of five Central American countries, called for termination of military aid to all insurgents, promotion of pluralistic, democratic systems, cease-fires, amnesties and dialogue between governments and unarmed opposition groups. President Ronald Reagan found the plan flawed, citing inadequate enforcement provisions. The plan faces its major test in Nicaragua, where the opposing sides agreed to cease fire and negotiate a peace settlement.

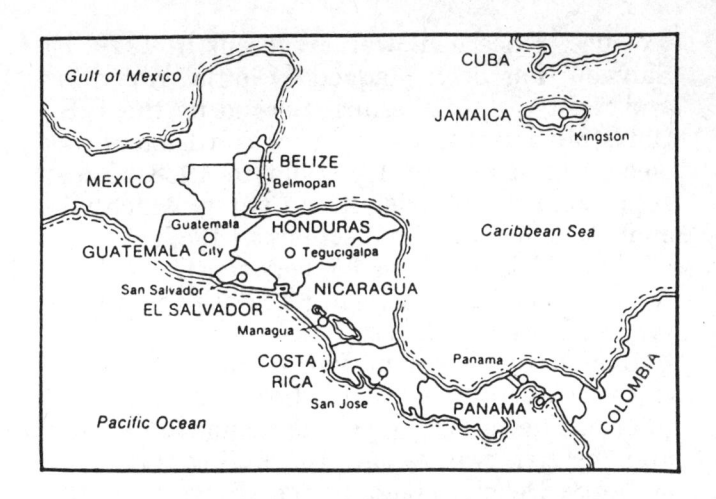

Guatemala. Except for a brief democratic interregnum that ended in a Central Intelligence Agency-backed coup in 1954, Guatemala has been ruled by the military. It has the worst human rights record in the Western Hemisphere, according to Amnesty International, which reported 100,000 people killed between 1966 and 1986, mostly by right-wing death squads and the military. Increasing guerrilla opposition to military rule and the government's ruthless response drove the U.S. in 1977 to condition further military aid on an improvement in Guatemala's human rights record. Guatemala in turn renounced the aid. Reagan persuaded Congress to vote limited aid in 1984, which was increased following the 1985 election of Christian Democrat Marco Vinicio Cerezo Arévalo. Since then, Cerezo's government has weathered a coup and relations with the U.S. have cooled due to his policy of "active neutrality" (refusal to oppose the Sandinistas).

El Salvador is the smallest, poorest, most densely populated country in Central America. In 1979, a civilian-military junta replaced a military dictatorship, bringing with it both social and economic reforms—and an increase in political violence. Since civil war broke out in 1979, El Salvador has been plagued by leftist guerrillas and right-wing vigilantes. Backed by the U.S., Christian Democrat José Napoleón Duarte was elected president in 1984, but in 1988 he lost support to the rightist Arena party, which will challenge his party in elections in 1989.

U.S. aid to El Salvador between fiscal years (FY) 1984 and 1987 totaled $1.47 billion for military and economic security assistance and $294 million for development. Part of the economic assistance is contingent on further progress in land reform. The country's serious economic troubles and the civil war remain continuing threats to stability. Despite civilian rule, analysts say the military remains the country's strongest institution. A signatory of the Guatemala accord, Duarte so far has made unsuccessful attempts to come to terms with the rebels.

Honduras emerged from a decade of military rule to twice elect Liberal presidents in the 1980s. José Azcona Hoyo has headed the country since 1986. Situated between Nicaragua and El Salvador, this country has been indirectly involved in both civil wars, and at the behest of the U.S. has allowed the Nicaraguan contras to establish camps on Honduran territory. The U.S. has over 1,000 troops stationed in Honduras and regularly runs joint U.S.-Honduran military exercises in the country. In Mar. 1988, following a Sandinista attack on the contras, Reagan dispatched 3,200 troops to central Honduras in response to a request for assistance. The U.S. considers Honduras its closest ally in Central America, despite recent tension surrounding growing Honduran impatience with the contras. From 1983 to 1987, Honduras received $321.9 million in U.S. military aid. Reports say that since it signed the peace plan, which requires it to expel the contras from its territory, the Honduran military have been cracking down on political opposition at the expense of human rights.

Nicaragua. Following 21 years of U.S. intervention, the Somoza family ruled Nicaragua, with one brief interlude, from 1934 until 1979, when a broad-based coalition, including the Sandinistas, overthrew the government. Within two years, the Marxist Sandinistas had alienated their democratic co-revolutionaries and consolidated their control of the government. Daniel Ortega Saavedra was elected president in 1984. Dissatisfied revolutionaries joined with former Somoza National Guardsmen in 1981 to form a guerrilla force currently calling itself the Nicaraguan Resistance, or contras.

Despite longtime U.S. backing of the Somozas, President Jimmy Carter proffered aid to the new Nicaraguan government. In 1981, however, the U.S. froze aid due to evidence the Sandinistas were helping the Salvadoran rebels. President Reagan made the cutoff permanent and began supporting the contras, who now number some 15,000. The Soviets supply military support as well as nearly 100% of the energy needs and other forms of aid to the Sandinistas.

Reagan's personal championship of the contras has made their funding a highly partisan and often volatile issue in Congress. U.S. policy has ranged from a freeze on all aid for fiscal year (FY) 1985 to a high of $100 million for military and humanitarian aid approved for FY 1987. Following the Iran-contra hearings of 1986–87 (see Chapter 1) revealing that members of the National Security Council staff had illegally channeled funds from Iranian arms sales to the contras, aid requests have met with greater public scrutiny.

On Mar. 24, 1988, shortly after the U.S. show of force in Honduras in support of the contras, the Sandinistas and the contras sat down for unprecedented peace talks. They agreed on terms for a cease-fire and subsequently held several rounds of negotiations. Nicaragua, in compliance with the peace plan, lifted some restrictions on the mass media and released some political prisoners. Critics call the measures inadequate while others applaud them as evidence of democratization.

By Brookins for *The Richmond Times-Dispatch*.

Costa Rica. Democratic and without an army since 1948, Costa Rica has long been an island of stability and neutrality in Central America. Its government, headed by Oscar Arias Sánchez since 1986, has taken the lead in bringing the Sandinistas and the contras to the negotiating table. Costa Rica's principal concerns are the presence of contras in the northern border area, increased U.S. involvement in Costa Rican affairs and an economy suffering under the strains of a large foreign debt, high oil prices and low coffee prices (the former an import, the latter an export).

Panama is of unique importance to the U.S. because of its status as the headquarters of the U.S. Southern Command, home to some 9,500 U.S. troops, and the Panama Canal. In 1977, treaties were signed turning over control of the Canal (a sea-lane for U.S. naval and merchant shipping) from U.S. to Panamanian administration in the year 2000.

Since a 1968 coup, Panama has been run by its military. In 1983, Gen. Manuel Antonio Noriega assumed control of the country, despite the facade of a civilian government. He reportedly fixed elections in 1984 to ensure a victory by his party's candidate. The president, pressured by Noriega, resigned one year later and handed the position

By Mike Peters for *The Dayton Daily News*.

over to his first vice-president, Eric Arturo Delvalle Henríquez. In Feb. 1988, following the disclosure of U.S. indictments of Noriega on drug trafficking charges and after consultation with the State Department, Delvalle demanded the general's resignation. He was fired and went into hiding. While Noriega continues to run the country, Delvalle is recognized abroad as Panama's legitimate head of state. Evidence of Noriega's corruption, alliance with drug traffickers and human rights abuses has outraged Panamanians as well as people in the U.S.

ADMINISTRATION POLICY

The Reagan Administration's Central American policy has centered on preventing the Soviets from gaining influence in the region. It sees the Marxist rebels in El Salvador and the pro-Soviet Sandinista government in Nicaragua as the main threats. Additional U.S. interests include combating the flow of drugs from and through these countries (see Chapter 7) and resolving the more recent political crisis in Panama.

Under the Reagan Doctrine, a policy intended to roll back Communist expansion by supporting anti-Communist movements, the Administration has supported the Nicaraguan contras and been cool toward the Guatemala peace plan. It alleges the plan strengthens the existing government in Nicaragua and imposes no penalties in the event of noncompliance. Enough members of Congress, however, liked the plan sufficiently to oppose any more military aid for the contras. On Mar. 31, 1988, they approved $48 million, exclusively in humanitarian aid, including $17.7 million each for the contras and for Nicaraguan children injured in the war.

Following the indictment of Panama's Gen. Noriega on charges of drug trafficking, the U.S. sought first to break the general's hold on power with economic pressure. It put U.S. Canal payments in escrow and ordered private U.S. entities to withhold taxes and other payments due the Panamanian government. Recognizing that this hurt the populace more than the government (40% of Panama's stores and businesses have gone bankrupt as a result) and confronted with Noriega's resistance, the U.S. retreated, allowing private firms to make some payments. In late May, U.S. diplomatic efforts to persuade Noriega to step down collapsed.

The U.S. provides aid to all of Central America except Nicaragua and, for the moment, Panama. Only El Salvador and Honduras receive more military than development support.

POLICY CHOICES

❐ The U.S. should cease all aid to the contras and support the Guatemala peace plan.
Yes. (1) The Nicaraguan government was elected by popular vote, and U.S. efforts to overthrow it violate Nicaraguan sovereignty and international law. (2) Continued aid to the contras perpetuates an unwinnable war that has cost 25,000 lives on both sides. (3) The peace plan, which is supported by the international community, offers the region its best chance for lasting peace.
No. (1) The Sandinistas will make Nicaragua a

Soviet stepping-stone in the Western Hemisphere, endangering national, even territorial, security. (2) The Nicaraguan freedom fighters can win the war if the U.S. is prepared to commit adequate resources. (3) Without continued U.S. pressure on the Sandinistas in the form of support for the contras, Nicaragua cannot be trusted to honor the Guatemala accord.

❒ The U.S. must protect its interests in Panama at all costs.
Yes. (1) U.S. merchant ships and the Navy depend on the Canal, and the U.S. must intervene, if necessary, to protect its interests. (2) Instability in Panama can spill over to the rest of Central America, with serious consequences for the U.S.
No. (1) The Canal is no longer the critical sea-lane it once was; it only accommodates relatively small ships. (2) The right to operate the Canal does not imply the right to select Panama's government.

❒ The U.S. should provide economic aid and end military aid to Central America.
Yes. (1) "You won't beat communism with arms but with an improvement of the economic and social conditions of the people" (Oscar Arias). (2) The military in Central America constitute the chief threat to democracy and economic progress.
No. (1) Central America's democratic governments need strong military capabilities to fend off Soviet- and Cuban-backed insurgencies. (2) The civilian governments must pacify their armed forces or risk even greater instability.

SELECT BIBLIOGRAPHY

"Changing Central America." *Current History,* Dec. 1987. Entire issue devoted to Central America.

Domínguez, Jorge I., and Lindenberg, Marc, "Central America: Current Crisis and Future Prospects." *Headline Series* No. 271. New York, Foreign Policy Association, Nov./Dec. 1984. An overview of the issues and U.S. options.

Fuentes, Carlos, "Who Is the Real Threat?" *World Press Review,* Apr. 1987, pp.24–25. A Mexican perspective on U.S. policy in Central America.

Nuccio, Richard A., *What's Wrong, Who's Right in Central America?* New York, Facts on File Publications, 1986. Background on the region and discussion of U.S. policies by the director of the Roosevelt Center's Latin American and Caribbean programs.

Reagan, Ronald, "Promoting Freedom and Democracy in Central America." *Department of State Bulletin,* July 1987, pp.1–4. Speech enunciating the Reagan Doctrine.

Robinson, Linda, "Peace in Central America." *Foreign Affairs,* Vol. 66, No. 3 *(America and the World 1987/88),* pp. 591–613. Narrative review of Central America's progress toward peace.

9

Middle East Flash Points

✔ *What role should the U.S. play in the Arab-Israeli peace process?*

✔ *What policies will best protect U.S. interests in the Persian Gulf?*

✔ *Can the U.S. help end the Iran-Iraq War?*

FACTS

- The Persian Gulf states possess 65% of the free world's oil reserves.
- In 1986, the Gulf region supplied 6% of the oil consumed by the U.S.; 60% of Japan's; 51% of Italy's; and 33% of France's.
- From 1981 through 1987, 446 ships, mainly oil tankers, have been attacked in the Gulf.
- In 1987, U.S. aid to Israel was $3 billion; to Egypt, $2.3 billion.

BACKGROUND

U.S. involvement in the Middle East was minor until World War II. Afterward, the U.S. replaced Britain and France as the main Western power and counterweight to Soviet influence. Major U.S. goals in the Middle East have included:
- containing Communist expansion,
- maintaining access to Persian Gulf oil,
- supporting Israel, and
- seeking oil concessions and promoting trade.

To fulfill these goals, U.S. Presidents have announced "doctrines" aimed at discouraging

Soviet involvement in the region and have proposed plans to resolve the Arab-Israeli dispute.

The Truman and Eisenhower Administrations were preoccupied with the Communist threat to the region and believed Arab nationalists, such as President Gamal Abdel Nasser of Egypt, were pro-Soviet. This was one reason the U.S. canceled an offer in 1956 to finance the Aswan Dam in Egypt. Nasser responded by nationalizing the Suez Canal. Britain and France invaded the canal area in retaliation following an Israeli invasion of Sinai. The foreign troops were forced to withdraw under U.S. and Soviet pressure.

Nasser's triumph in the Suez war was a watershed for the Middle East. In the face of Arab nationalism and a growing Soviet economic and military presence, U.S. influence among Arab states declined. U.S. ties with the non-Arab states (Turkey, Iran and Pakistan) along the region's Northern Tier, however, remained strong. These countries, along with Britain and Iraq, made up the U.S.-supported Baghdad Pact of 1955, which, after Iraq's withdrawal in 1959, became the Central Treaty Organization (CENTO).

ARAB-ISRAELI CONFLICT

Conflict between Israel and its Arab neighbors has so far resulted in five wars: Israel's war of independence (1948), the Suez war (1956), the Six-Day War (1967), the October war (1973) and the Israeli invasion of Lebanon (1982).

The June 1967 war, which Nasser provoked by forcing the withdrawal of United Nations forces, sending Egyptian troops into Sinai and preventing shipping from reaching the Israeli port of Eilat, ended in a stunning Israeli victory. Israel tripled the size of its territory by taking the West Bank and East Jerusalem from Jordan; Sinai and the Gaza Strip from Egypt; and the Golan Heights from Syria.

Afterward, the U.S. came to regard Israel as

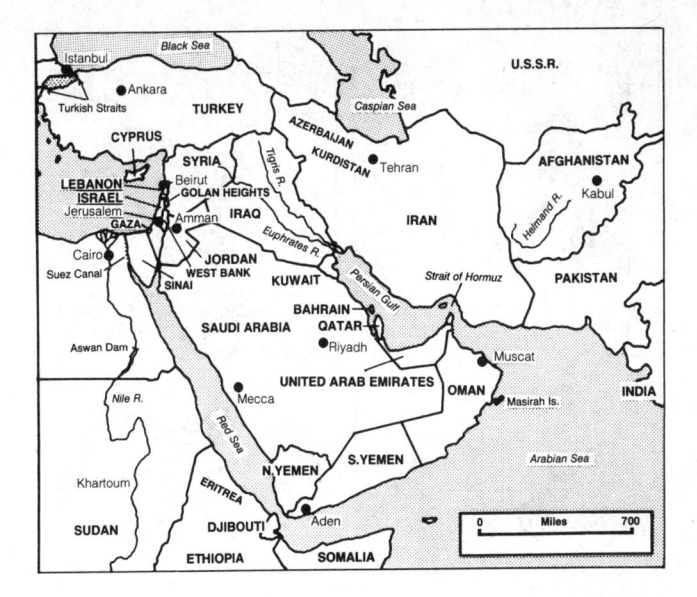

the guardian of U.S. interests and a reliable, democratic ally in an unstable region. The U.S. has been Israel's main arms supplier since then, and a major aid donor.

Egypt and Syria struck back in a surprise attack on Israel in Oct. 1973. While Israel prevailed militarily, the Arab armies performed creditably and gained a renewed sense of confidence and power.

Search for solutions. A widely accepted formula for settling the Arab-Israeli dispute is contained in UN Resolution 242, passed on Nov. 22, 1967. The resolution calls on Israel to withdraw from territories occupied in 1967 in return for its acceptance by its Arab neighbors, including the right to live in peace within secure and recognized borders.

After the 1973 war, Secretary of State Henry Kissinger negotiated troop disengagement agreements and made Middle East peace a top U.S. goal. Egypt, which had expelled Soviet advisers in 1972, turned to the West for help; the U.S. instituted a massive aid program.

The greatest advance toward peace was made through the mediation of U.S. President Jimmy

> "I'M A PALESTINIAN NATIONALIST" — "DEPORT HIM!" SHAMIR
>
> "I'M A PALESTINIAN EDITOR" — "SILENCE HIM!"
>
> "I'M A PALESTINIAN STUDENT LEADER" — "DETAIN HER!"
>
> "WE'RE WILLING TO NEGOTIATE WITH THE PALESTINIANS... ...BUT THERE'S NO ONE TO TALK TO"

Wasserman © 1988, *The Boston Globe*.

Carter with Egyptian President Anwar al-Sadat and Israeli Prime Minister Menachem Begin. Agreements reached at Camp David, Md., in Sept. 1978 led Egypt to sign a peace treaty with Israel in Mar. 1979, in defiance of other Arab states, and led Israel to complete its return of the Sinai to Egypt in 1982. The U.S. has provided large-scale aid to the two countries ever since, and still participates in a peacekeeping force in Sinai.

The Palestinians. The Camp David accords did not successfully address the future of the 5 million Palestinians. The accords provided for a five-year period of self-rule in the West Bank and Gaza, during which the permanent status of the inhabitants, primarily Palestinians, was to be negotiated by Israel, Egypt and Jordan. So far Israel has not permitted the local elections envisioned in the accords to take place. Palestinians, who reject the Camp David accords, demand their own state; Israel has refused to permit this.

Many Arab states, including Egypt and Jordan, now believe the Camp David formula for settling the future of the occupied territories must be revised. They favor holding an international peace conference under the auspices of the

The PLO Post
1970-1999 Edition
Good for 30 Years
Buy once, read it every day
Militant Stance Upheld
Palestinian Question Not Resolved
Some Unity Reported
Disagreements Remain
Nothing Settled
Solution Years Away
ARAFAT
Arafat's Beard Now Two Days Old
I'M ASKED ALL THE TIME. THE ANSWER IS HEDGE CLIPPERS!

By Toles, Universal Press Syndicate.

five permanent members of the UN Security Council (the U.S., U.S.S.R., Britain, France and China). Foreign Minister Shimon Peres of Israel also backs this approach; however, Prime Minister Yitzhak Shamir is opposed, fearful that at a conference Israel's enemies would "gang up" and seek to impose an unacceptable solution.

A major stumbling block is agreeing on who would represent the Palestinians at such a conference. At a 1974 summit meeting, Arab leaders declared the Palestine Liberation Organization (PLO), founded in 1964 as an umbrella organization for Palestinian groups, to be the "sole legitimate representative" of the Palestinian people. The U.S. and Israel refuse to negotiate with the PLO until it recognizes Israel and forswears terrorism. A solution acceptable to the U.S. would be to let Jordan's King Hussein negotiate on the Palestinians' behalf, but he refuses to do so unless an Arab consensus backs him up.

The uprising. Anti-Israeli protests by rock-throwing Palestinian youths have taken place in the West Bank and Gaza since Dec. 1987 and have refocused attention on the Palestinians' dilemma. (By 1985, there were 3.5 million Jews and 2.1 million Arabs living in Israel and the occupied territories.) The demonstrations have enhanced the prestige of the PLO and its leader, Yasir Arafat.

The riots prompted a harsh Israeli crackdown in which 170 Palestinians had been killed by late May 1988. Prime Minister Shamir characterized the uprising as a war "against Israelis, against the existence of the state of Israel." Others regard the uprising as a sign of desperation on the part of Palestinians who see no peaceful end to two decades of Israeli occupation.

THE PERSIAN GULF

After the British had withdrawn from the Gulf in 1971, the U.S. depended on the shah of Iran to keep the oil flowing and exclude Soviet influence. This fitted in with the Nixon Doctrine of having regional powers assume greater responsibility for collective security.

This policy fell apart after the Iranian revolution began in early 1978. The ouster of the shah by

By Ohman. Reprinted by permission, Tribune Media Services.

militant Shiite Muslims under the banner of Ayatollah Ruhollah Khomeini, the taking of American hostages and the Soviet invasion of Afghanistan were strategic setbacks for the U.S. The Jan. 1980 Carter Doctrine warned that a Soviet attempt to gain control of the Persian Gulf region would be repelled with military force if necessary.

Iraq's attack on Iran in Sept. 1980 led to a war which has threatened the security of Gulf oil supplies and the survival of moderate regional leaders. The war remains stalemated despite a number of major Iranian offensives, Iraqi use of chemical weapons and great loss of life on both sides. Iraq has offered to negotiate an end to the war; Iran has refused Iraq's terms. The Soviet Union says it wants the war to end, but has sold arms to both sides and has not endorsed a UN resolution to impose an arms embargo on Iran.

ADMINISTRATION POLICY

Arab-Israeli peace. The Reagan Administration, compared with its predecessors, has been relatively uninvolved in the peace process. In Sept. 1982 President Ronald Reagan proposed a plan giving Palestinians on the West Bank and Gaza self-government in association with Jordan, but ruled out a Palestinian state. He also called on Israel not to build any more settlements on the West Bank. Israel and Syria rejected the plan, however, and Jordan did not fully go along. Despite the fact that others regard the U.S. proposal as moribund, the Administration maintains it is still the basis for U.S. diplomacy.

In 1988, the U.S. initiated a new peace effort in an attempt to defuse growing violence in the occupied territories. Secretary of State George P. Shultz traveled to the region and outlined a proposal calling for an international conference (with no power to impose or veto solutions) and local elections leading to self-administration for the

West Bank and Gaza, followed by negotiations on the final status of the territories based on the principle of land for peace.

The most problematic aspect of the plan is how it treats the Palestinians. They would be represented only as part of a joint delegation with Jordan, although King Hussein, in a policy switch, now declares that they must speak for themselves. Palestinians refused to meet with Shultz on his visits. Although Egypt offered support, no regional country fully accepted the plan, and Shamir has long rejected the idea of a conference.

Shultz appeared reluctant to pressure Shamir, although in Mar., 30 U.S. senators wrote to Shultz supporting his diplomatic efforts and criticizing Shamir for obstructing a peace settlement. In Apr., the U.S. and Israel signed a five-year agreement, long sought by Israel, formalizing their cooperation on a wide range of issues. With presidential elections scheduled for Nov. in both the U.S. and Israel, it was uncertain whether any diplomatic effort could be sustained.

Persian Gulf. Publicly stated U.S. policy toward the Iran-Iraq War under both the Carter and Reagan Administrations has been based on neutrality, support for the territorial integrity and political independence of both countries, encouragement of mediation efforts, and refusal to sell weapons to either side. The Reagan Administration branded Iran a terrorist state in Jan. 1984 and declared it would not deal with it.

However, the Iran-contra investigations, beginning in the fall of 1986, disclosed that the President, hoping to ransom American hostages held in Lebanon, had acquiesced in Israeli arms shipments to Iran as well as sanctioned direct U.S. arms transfers. Some of the proceeds were diverted to help the rebels (known as contras) fighting the Sandinista government in Nicaragua (see Chapter 10).

The new revelations showed that the U.S.—regarded as tilting toward Iraq since late 1983—had actually aided both sides. The U.S. government now insists it has reverted to its earlier stated policy of not dealing with Iran.

Current conflict. In order to reassure Arab governments in the Gulf, who were afraid the U.S. would not protect them from Iran, and to guarantee freedom of navigation, the Administration agreed to Kuwait's request to place 11 of its oil tankers under U.S. protection by "reflagging" them. This commitment led the U.S. to send a large naval task force to the Gulf beginning in July 1987. The U.S. requested assistance from its allies in the North Atlantic Treaty Organization, who agreed after initial resistance. By May 1988, there were 27 U.S. ships and 32 European ships deployed in the Gulf.

Arab governments welcomed the international armada, and the U.S. secured the closer defense cooperation with the Gulf states it had long sought. However, those states, with the exception of Bahrain and Oman, have not permitted the U.S. to establish military facilities on their territory.

Arms sales have traditionally been a major source of U.S. influence on Arab states. The Reagan Administration, however, has found it difficult to get congressional approval for such sales. This is especially true in an election year, when congressmen are loathe to do anything that could be interpreted as jeopardizing Israel's security.

U.S. policy in the Gulf—expanded in Apr. 1988 to include protection for neutral merchant vessels—at first was widely questioned in Congress. Many feared U.S. sailors had been sent to a war zone with no clear mission and believed the War Powers Resolution should be invoked, although no measures limiting the U.S. role were enacted. U.S. ships seemed inviting targets for Iranian mines and attacks from small boats. The cost to the U.S. was also considerable, by one estimate amounting to $365 million for 1987 alone.

Despite the U.S. presence, the "tanker war" between Iran and Iraq continued, with a record 174 ships attacked in 1987. The U.S.S. *Stark* was "inadvertently" attacked by Iraq on May 17, 1987, with a loss of 37 lives. On Apr. 18, 1988, U.S. and Iranian forces clashed in the Gulf, with the U.S. destroying two Iranian oil platforms and crippling or sinking six Iranian vessels. Two U.S. airmen were lost. Oil traffic in the Persian Gulf has not been halted and oil prices remain depressed.

The Administration believes that UN action offers the most promising way to end the war. In July 1987 the UN Security Council unanimously ordered a cease-fire, and since then the U.S. has pushed for the imposition of a global arms embargo on Iran. So far the Soviets (who depend on Iran's cooperation during their withdrawal from Afghanistan and who hope to preserve their influence in Iran in the future) and the Chinese (who are major arms suppliers to Iran) have refused to go along. Administration critics complain that the U.S. should exert more pressure on Iraq to end the war.

POLICY CHOICES

❏ The U.S. should withdraw from the Gulf.
Yes. (1) U.S. intervention has increased tension and led to more attacks on Gulf shipping than before. (2) The countries that benefit most from Gulf oil should protect it. (3) The U.S. cannot afford the cost.
No. (1) The U.S. has achieved its goal of guaranteeing oil exports and protecting freedom of navigation. (2) The intervention has bolstered U.S. credibility with Arab states. (3) U.S. policy has succeeded in limiting the Soviet presence in the Gulf.

❏ The U.S. should pressure Israel to end its occupation of the West Bank and Gaza.
Yes. (1) The U.S. has long upheld the principle of self-determination and should apply it in the case of the Palestinians. (2) Israel reneged on its prom-

ise, at Camp David, to permit autonomy, local elections and a negotiated solution.

No. (1) Israel knows best its security needs. The U.S. should not interfere. (2) The Palestinians should give up terrorism and accept the state of Israel before Israel makes concessions to them.

SELECT BIBLIOGRAPHY

Bill, James A., "The Shah, the Ayatollah and the U.S." *Headline Series* No. 285. New York, Foreign Policy Association, June 1988. Story of the complex relationship and foreign policy errors that led to the Iran-contra affair.

The Middle East, 6th ed. Washington, D.C., Congressional Quarterly, 1986. Excellent overview of U.S. policy and current issues.

Toward Arab-Israeli Peace: Report of a Study Group. Washington, D.C., The Brookings Institution, 1988. Outlines a role for the U.S.

"U.S. and the Middle East: Dangerous Drift?" *Great Decisions 1988.* New York, Foreign Policy Association, 1988, pp. 49–61. Reviews changes in the region and in U.S. policy since World War II.

"U.S. Policy in the Persian Gulf." *Department of State Bulletin,* Oct. 1987, pp. 38–44. Historical overview and current U.S. policy.

10

Southern Africa in Turmoil

✔ *How can the U.S. show its support for blacks in South Africa?*

✔ *Should the U.S. continue aiding the rebels in Angola?*

✔ *Should the U.S. provide aid to Mozambique?*

BACKGROUND

The European colonization of southern Africa began with Portuguese merchants in search of slaves and a route to India in the late 15th century. The Dutch East India Company followed in the mid-17th century, and Britain captured the Cape of Good Hope at the end of the 18th century. A century later Britons in search of gold and diamonds flocked to southern Africa. Competition between British and Afrikaners (descendants of the Dutch) for land and resources led to the Boer War (1899–1902). The Afrikaners lost; their colonies were merged with Britain's to form the Union of South Africa, which became an independent state in 1934.

Since World War II, all the nations of southern Africa except South-West Africa have achieved independence. (South Africa's League of Nations mandate over South-West Africa, now known as Namibia, was revoked by the United Nations in 1966. Since then, South Africa has occupied Namibia illegally.)

South Africa is the only independent state controlled by its white minority. Whites make up

The countries compared:	Population (millions) (mid-1985)	Average annual growth of pop. (%) (1980–85)	Infant mortality (per 1,000)	Life expectancy at birth (1985)	GNP per capita ($U.S.) (1985)
Angola	8.8	2.5	143	44	n.a.
Botswana	1.1	3.5	71	57	840
Lesotho	1.5	2.7	106	54	470
Malawi	7.0	3.1	156	45	170
Mozambique	13.8	3.3	123	47	160
Namibia	1.1	2.7	110	49	1,250
South Africa	32.4	2.5	78	55	2,010
Swaziland	0.8	n.a.	n.a.	54	670
Tanzania	22.2	3.5	110	52	290
Zaire	30.6	3.0	102	51	170
Zambia	6.7	3.5	84	52	390
Zimbabwe	8.4	3.7	77	57	680

Sources: *The World Bank Atlas 1987* and *World Development Report 1987*, prepared by The World Bank.

16% of the population, blacks—as defined by South Africa—the rest, including Africans (72%), coloreds, or people of mixed race (9%), and Asians (3%). Since it came to power in 1948, the Afrikaner-led National party has used apartheid—strict racial separation and discrimination legally mandated and enforced through a system of police repression—to maintain minority control. Between 1960 and 1980, more than 3 million Africans were forcibly relocated to 10 "homelands" (each territory purportedly the home of a different African tribe). Homelands have only 14% of South Africa's territory, much of it desolate.

International opposition. The UN General Assembly addressed apartheid for the first time in 1952; South Africa challenged UN jurisdiction over "an exclusively domestic matter." The world condemned the 1960 Sharpeville massacre of blacks. In 1963 the UN Security Council, with

U.S. support, approved a voluntary embargo on arms shipments to South Africa. South Africa was suspended from the UN General Assembly in 1974. After South Africa's military intervention in the Angolan civil war in 1975–76, its repression of the 1976 Soweto riots, and the suspicious death of black leader Steven Biko, the Security Council in 1977 voted a mandatory arms embargo.

Adapt or die? President P.W. Botha told his fellow Afrikaners in 1979 that they must "adapt or die." To that end, he granted some union rights to blacks that year and repealed many of the laws of "petty apartheid." Reforms included the repeal of the Prohibition of Mixed Marriages Act of 1949; the amendment of the Black Communities Development Act of 1984, granting permission for blacks to acquire property in urban areas designated for them; the Abolition of Influx Control Act of 1986, which abolished passbooks and replaced them with uniform identity documents. The reforms reduced some officially mandated apartheid without endangering white control of the political and economic system.

In Nov. 1983, the all-white electorate by a 2–1 margin approved a new constitution, creating a tricameral legislature with one house for whites, one for coloreds, one for Asians—and none for Africans.

Recent developments. Following widespread antiapartheid demonstrations, documented on foreign television screens, the government declared a state of emergency in June 1986 and reimposed strict censorship of media coverage of unrest. The restrictions remain in effect.

In May 1987 elections for the white chamber of Parliament, the ruling National party won only 52% of the vote; the Conservative party, which wants to restore full apartheid, won over 25% and displaced the more moderate Progressive Federal party as the official opposition. The Conservatives made another strong showing in two Mar. 1988 by-elections.

Aug. 9–30, 1987: Although a strike by more

than 250,000 black mine workers eventually collapsed, its staying power surprised management.

Feb. 24, 1988: The government severely restricted the political activities of 17 leading black opposition groups and the country's largest labor federation. The U.S. State Department called it a "giant step backward."

Apr. 21, 1988: President Botha raised the possibility of giving blacks a voice in the national government and creating black urban councils.

Economic sanctions. In autumn 1986, the U.S. Congress imposed economic sanctions against South Africa, following a similar action by the 49 members of the Commonwealth and the 12-member European Community (EC). Passed over President Ronald Reagan's veto, the legislation bans imports of South African uranium, coal, steel, iron, textiles and agricultural products. It also forbids new U.S. loans and investments.

In 1987 public demand for stronger pressure

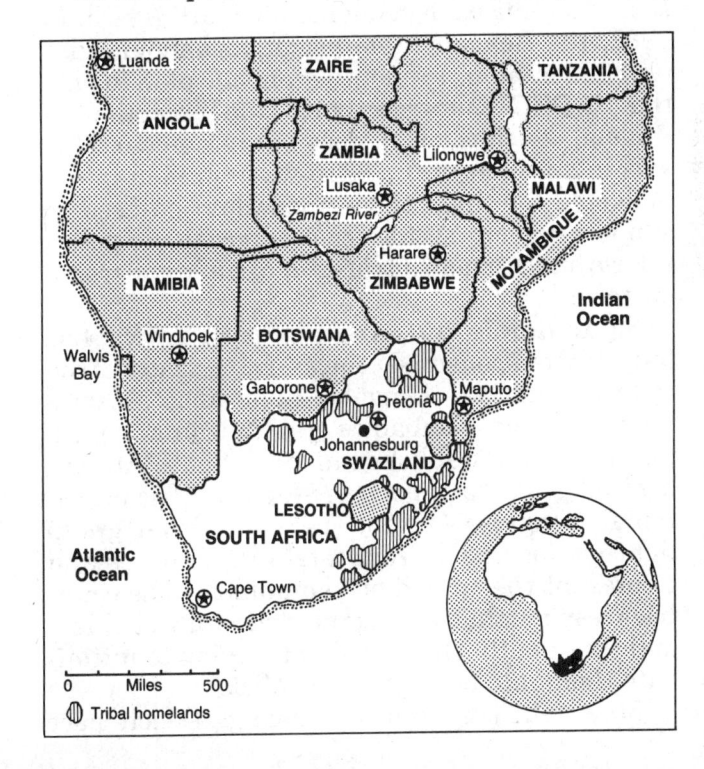

against South Africa grew, with calls for shareholders to divest their stock in corporations doing business in South Africa and for U.S. corporations in South Africa to disinvest, that is, sell their assets. Since 1986, 104 U.S. companies have stopped doing business in South Africa; 160 remain.

A region overshadowed. The Republic of South Africa dominates the region of southern Africa, economically and militarily. At least 50% to 60% of the trade of Malawi, Zambia and Zimbabwe is dependent on South Africa's transportation system. There are some 1 million workers in South Africa from neighboring nations; their salaries support some 5 million dependents.

In 1980, Angola, Botswana, Lesotho, Malawi, Mozambique, Swaziland, Tanzania, Zambia and Zimbabwe formed the Southern African Development Coordination Conference (SADCC), an instrument for closer regional economic cooperation and reduced dependence on South Africa. In 1987, the Reagan Administration announced a new $93 million, 18-month economic plan to help the SADCC countries (with the exception of Angola, which the U.S. does not recognize). This was in addition to the $210–$245 million in aid budgeted for that region and would be used to support private sector-oriented economic policy reform and promote intraregional trade and transportation.

Apartheid's outreach. South Africa has launched or sponsored attacks against most of the frontline nations (Angola, Botswana, Mozambique, Zambia, Zimbabwe and Tanzania), an informal group established in 1974. South Africa's avowed goals have been to stop the African National Congress (ANC), the main rebel group fighting apartheid, from establishing bases and to prevent the spread of communism. The countries respond that most of the victims are civilians and that South Africa is simply trying to intimidate them into bowing to its policies.

Mozambique signed a nonaggression pact

with South Africa—the Nkomati Accord—in 1984, but in 1985 Mozambique charged South Africa with violating it by continuing to support the Mozambique National Resistance (Renamo). Mozambique is forced to spend 42% of its national budget to defend itself from the right-wing rebels. In Apr. 1988 the State Department reported that Renamo had killed at least 100,000 people and driven almost 1 million people into exile. The U.S. government has targeted $15 million in economic aid for Marxist Mozambique, which has suffered grave food shortages.

Namibia. In 1978 UN Security Council Resolution 435 called for the "early independence of Namibia through free elections." A South African administrator general runs Namibia with an occupying force of 120,000. South Africa has repeatedly postponed UN-supervised elections, many believe because it knows that the winner would be the South-West African People's Organization (SWAPO—a black Namibian independence movement with military bases in Angola).

Angola. Cuban troops have been stationed in Angola since 1975, following the outbreak of civil war after Angola won independence from Portugal. At that time, the new Marxist government requested Cuban protection against the National Union for the Total Independence of Angola (Unita), a South Africa-backed guerrilla force. At times, Unita has occupied as much as one third of Angola. In 1985 Congress repealed the Clark Amendment, banning support for the Angolan rebels, and since then has approved some $15 million a year in covert aid to Unita. According to the State Department, Angola received about $1 billion in arms from the Soviet Union in 1987.

ADMINISTRATION POLICY

The Reagan Administration condemns apartheid, but argues that change will be brought about not by economic sanctions but by "constructive engagement." During the last two years, however, the Administration has amended this policy. In an effort to improve communications with South Africa's blacks, in Oct. 1986 Washington sent a black ambassador, Edward J. Perkins, to South Africa. In Jan. 1987, Secretary of State George P. Shultz met in Washington with Oliver Tambo, ANC president. An advisory committee on South Africa reported to the Secretary of State the same month that "constructive engagement has failed," "a new policy is now urgently required" and that the Administration's main priority should be to strengthen ties with blacks.

The Administration continues to see South Africa as one part of a regional problem. It links Namibian independence with the removal of Cuban troops in Angola. In May 1988, the U.S. chaired a historic meeting in London of Angolan, Cuban and South African officials to work out a peace package. Discussions were also held at the May summit in Moscow, where the U.S. and Soviet Union set a Sept. target for working out a plan providing for Cuban and South African troop withdrawals, linked to the formation of a government of national reconciliation in Angola and independence for Namibia. Consistent with the Reagan Doctrine, which calls upon the U.S. to provide assistance to anti-Communist movements all over the world, the Administration supports Unita and considers continued aid nonnegotiable. The Administration has also given aid to the Marxist government of Mozambique and the other members of SADCC.

POLICY CHOICES

❏ The U.S. should support international sanctions against South Africa.
Yes. (1) Sanctions imposed unilaterally are ineffective. For example, the coal South Africa can no longer sell to the U.S. it sells to the EC. (2) The reforms South Africa has made are due to inter-

national pressure; more coordinated pressure would increase the pace. (3) By joining in international sanctions, the U.S. will enhance its standing among blacks and Third World nations.
No. (1) Sanctions are not working. White South Africans have bought up the businesses American companies have left behind, and black unemployment is up. (2) The U.S. has a strategic interest in stability in South Africa that only whites can ensure. (3) The best chance for change and black advancement in South Africa is through economic growth, which is hurt by sanctions.

❐ The U.S. should strengthen ties with the ANC.
Yes. (1) U.S. support will encourage the ANC; U.S. opposition is likely to radicalize the ANC and increase its dependence on Soviet aid. (2) U.S. sympathy for black rule would give Washington more leverage in a postapartheid South African society.
No. (1) The ANC advocates terrorism, which the U.S. cannot condone. (2) Instead of conferring credibility on the ANC, the U.S. should improve its ties with moderate blacks.

❐ The U.S. should continue to support Angola's Unita.
Yes. The U.S. has a responsibility to assist freedom fighters trying to overthrow a Marxist government and its Cuban protectors.
No. U.S. aid to the South African-supported guerrillas destabilizes Angola, damages U.S. standing with black Africans and sends South Africa the wrong signals.

SELECT BIBLIOGRAPHY

Baker, Pauline H., "South Africa: The Afrikaner Angst." *Foreign Policy,* Winter 1987–88, pp. 61–79. Why white South Africans are fragmented.

Mugabe, Robert G., "Struggle for Southern Africa."

Foreign Affairs, Winter 1987/88, pp. 311–27. Zimbabwe's prime minister urges stronger U.S. measures against South Africa.

Shultz, George P., "Southern Africa: American Hopes for the Future." *Department of State Bulletin,* Feb. 1987, pp. 36–40. The case for regional solutions.

"South Africa: Apartheid Under Siege." *Great Decisions 1987.* New York, Foreign Policy Association, 1987, pp. 45–54. Overview of South Africa's domestic and foreign relations.

11

The Atlantic Alliance

✔ *Does the alliance still serve U.S. needs and interests?*
✔ *Will the INF agreement weaken NATO?*
✔ *What future role should the U.S. play in NATO?*

FACTS

- Secretary-general of the North Atlantic Treaty Organization (NATO): Manfred Wörner (West Germany)
- Supreme Allied Commander Europe: Gen. John Galvin (U.S.)
- Defense expenditures of NATO's 16 members as percentage of gross domestic product (GDP), 1985

Greece	(7.1)	Norway	(3.1)
U.S.	(6.9)	Belgium	(2.9)
Britain	(5.2)	Italy	(2.7)
Turkey	(4.5)	Canada	(2.2)
France	(4.1)	Denmark	(2.2)
West Germany	(3.2)	Spain	(2.2)
Portugal	(3.2)	Luxembourg	(0.9)
Netherlands	(3.1)	Iceland	(0.0)

Source: International Institute for Strategic Studies, *The Military Balance, 1987–88.*

BACKGROUND

NATO was formed in 1949 to protect Western Europe against Soviet attack or intimidation. The NATO treaty provides that "an armed attack against one...shall be considered an attack against...all," and that each signatory will act to assist any victim of aggression as it deems necessary, "including the use of armed force." Of the 12 original signatories, only the U.S., with its nuclear monopoly, was militarily and economically strong enough after World War II to afford such protection to its allies. American nuclear weapons and the presence of U.S. troops (there are currently over 325,000 on European soil) served to reassure Europe of the U.S. commitment. Today Western Europe is a more equal partner—and sometimes rival—of the U.S.

NATO's strongest and most important European members are Britain, France and West Germany, who are also core members of the European Economic Community (EEC, or Common Market), a free-trade zone with a common agricultural policy and external tariff that today is the world's largest trading bloc. Britain is this country's closest ally. Its policies under British Prime Minister Margaret Thatcher (1979–) have coincided far more often than not with those of the Reagan Administration. France, although it withdrew from NATO's military command (but not from the alliance's political councils) in 1966, has remained committed to a strong national defense under President François Mitterrand. Britain and France are the only two West European nations with their own nuclear weapons. West Germany, Western Europe's most populous and prosperous country, is prohibited by the 1954 agreement that led to its statehood (as well as the nuclear nonproliferation treaty, which it has signed) from acquiring its own nuclear weapons. Closest to Eastern Europe, West Germany plays a pivotal alliance role.

Although there has been peace in Europe for four decades, West Europeans and Americans periodically question whether NATO continues to serve their interests. There have been perennial strains over East-West relations, policies toward the Third World, economic issues and nuclear strategy. Some West Europeans are questioning the strength of the U.S. commitment to the alliance; some U.S. critics think NATO's structure should be reformed to give Europeans more responsibility for their own defense.

East-West relations. West Europeans benefited greatly from the years of reduced tensions, or *détente,* between East and West, which peaked in the early 1970s. But when Americans became disenchanted with détente and expected their European allies to follow their lead in hardening their stand toward the U.S.S.R., a series of political and economic disputes followed. Most serious among these was the pipeline dispute of 1981-82, triggered when the Reagan Administration barred European companies licensed by the U.S. from fulfilling contracts with the Soviet Union to provide materials for a natural gas pipeline from Siberia to Western Europe. The U.S. eventually backed down.

Third World. Europeans and Americans have also disagreed on policies toward regions outside of the North Atlantic area, where their interests are often divergent. In the Middle East, for example, Americans have frequently been frustrated by European unwillingness to support U.S. policies for fear of antagonizing the Arabs who supply them with most of their oil. In 1973, some NATO members refused overflight permission to the U.S. in its effort to resupply Israel during the October war. NATO members currently share in the protection of international shipping in the Persian Gulf; initially, however, NATO defense ministers resisted the U.S. call for help. To Americans, such lack of cooperation often seems like ingratitude toward a generous protector.

Economic issues. European economies are

greatly affected by what happens in the U.S., and European governments often disagree with U.S. economic policies. Areas of contention have included high U.S. interest rates and an overvalued dollar. In Oct. 1987, European markets crashed following the 500-point drop on the New York Stock Exchange, which many Europeans blamed on the large U.S. Federal budget deficit. The U.S., in turn, is frequently unhappy with European economic policies, for example West Germany's reluctance to loosen control of its money supply and EEC protectionism.

Military strategy. NATO's military strategy has been based since 1967 on deterrence through "flexible response": that is, the alliance maintains the capability to respond to Soviet aggression at whatever level it occurs—from a conventional attack to an intercontinental-range nuclear strike. In the mid-1970s, some Europeans grew concerned over growing numbers of Soviet SS–20s, intermediate-range nuclear missiles, aimed at Western Europe. (Intermediate-range nuclear forces, or INF, have a range of 300–3,400 miles.) In response, NATO adopted the "dual track" decision of 1979, pledging to deploy U.S. Pershing IIs and cruise missiles in Europe unless the Soviets removed their SS–20s and other INF. The Soviets walked out of arms control negotiations in late 1983 when deployment of the U.S. INF began over the protests of a large, vocal minority in several European countries.

Reykjavik and the INF agreement. In Oct. 1986, President Ronald Reagan and Soviet leader Mikhail S. Gorbachev met in Reykjavik, Iceland. There they discussed removing not only both sides' INF, but also eliminating their strategic nuclear systems within 10 years, reducing nuclear testing and halting the proliferation of chemical weapons. Although the talks ended without agreement, the European NATO allies, who had not been consulted beforehand, were alarmed by the turn the talks had taken. They feared that the elimination of U.S. nuclear weapons might be the first step toward an American withdrawal from Europe.

The U.S. consulted extensively with its allies following Reykjavik. When the treaty eliminating U.S. and Soviet INF was eventually signed in Dec. 1987, West European governments and publics strongly supported it. But Reykjavik and the INF treaty raised several serious issues.

The conventional balance. Although some 4,000 short-range as well as airborne and seaborne nuclear weapons are unaffected by the agreement, the elimination of an entire class of nuclear weapons has heightened concern over the imbalance in conventional forces in Europe. By most counts, the nonnuclear forces (men, tanks, artillery, etc.) of the Warsaw Pact, the Soviet-East European military alliance, outnumber NATO's. However, numerical inferiority does not necessarily translate into a NATO military disadvantage; many military analysts think NATO has an edge in some technology, quality of leadership and training, alliance cohesion and other factors.

Burden-sharing. Conventional weapons are much more expensive in terms of "bang for the buck" than nuclear weapons, which poses a problem since allies on both sides of the Atlantic are feeling a budgetary pinch. Until now, the U.S. has been paying a much larger share of NATO defense costs (69%) than its allies and has devoted a far higher percentage of its GDP to defense. Europeans make other substantial contributions, including 90% of NATO troops in Europe, over 80% of combat naval ships, and roughly half of NATO's tanks, artillery and aircraft. No European NATO member has lived up to a 1977 pledge to increase annual real defense spending by 3%, and it is unlikely that they will in the near future.

The structure of the alliance. Those who think that the current alliance structure is inequitable or unworkable have put forth two basic types of proposals for reform. One, known as devolution, would shift more financial responsibility for defense onto European shoulders, while keeping the U.S. actively involved in the alliance. The other, disengagement, calls for U.S. withdrawal from NATO, leaving Europeans on their own.

Worries about the firmness of the U.S. commitment to NATO since Reykjavik have prompted Europeans to talk more seriously about building a credible European defense within NATO. In the fall of 1987, France and West Germany formed a joint army brigade and joint defense council. France has also begun discussing coordination of nuclear targeting strategies with Britain. The long-inactive Western European Union (Belgium, Britain, France, Italy, Luxembourg, the Netherlands and West Germany) also seems to have revived, with its members in Oct. 1987 pledging closer cooperation on security matters.

ADMINISTRATION POLICY

The Reagan Administration has resisted any suggestion that the U.S. lessen its involvement in NATO, while emphasizing the need for greater European contributions to NATO conventional forces. The U.S. has assured the West Europeans that it will help maintain their security regardless of the outcome of arms negotiations with the Soviet Union (see Chapter 2). The U.S. Joint Chiefs of Staff, after initial reservations, backed the INF treaty and are studying ways to adjust U.S. military strategy and force levels to compensate for the missiles that will be eliminated. Military measures under consideration include modernization of short-range nuclear weapons based in West Germany, basing more nuclear-capable aircraft (not covered by the treaty) in Europe, and making some U.S. strategic weapons available for NATO missions.

The Administration wants conventional forces built up and modernized, while it continues negotiating with the Soviet Union on reducing the level of nonnuclear arms. However, lower levels of U.S. defense spending and the need to divert resources to other parts of the world may in fact require at least some cutbacks in Europe. A study conducted by the Joint Chiefs of Staff in late 1987 concluded that even without U.S. INF or a conventional buildup, a Soviet attack on Europe is highly unlikely.

POLICY CHOICES

❐ The U.S. should build up conventional forces in Europe.
Yes. (1) A conventional buildup is necessary to maintain the East-West military balance once INF are eliminated. (2) A buildup is necessary to give the Soviet Union an incentive to negotiate reductions in conventional arsenals.
No. (1) Despite the disparity in numbers, there is no significant East-West conventional imbalance in Europe, so a conventional buildup is unnecessary. (2) A U.S. conventional buildup is politically unattainable at a time when the American public favors cutting defense costs.

❐ The U.S. should give European NATO members more responsibility for their own defense.
Yes. (1) Increased European financial and decisionmaking responsibility would eliminate some of the sources of transatlantic tension. (2) Greater responsibility would lead to greater defense coordination among European nations, resulting in improved efficiency.
No. (1) Without strong U.S. leadership, Europeans will not be able to unite and coordinate defense planning. (2) In the absence of U.S. leadership, Moscow will chip away at alliance cohesion and may persuade some members to adopt a more neutral political and military posture.

❐ The U.S. should begin withdrawing some of its forces from Europe.
Yes. (1) The U.S. can no longer afford to defend every region in the world and must choose those

that are the most vital. (2) The threat to withdraw men and resources should be used to convince Western Europe to give greater support to U.S. policies toward both the Soviet bloc and the Third World.

No. (1) Western Europe is still an area of vital interest to the U.S. If the U.S. were to begin withdrawing its forces, Europe and the Soviet Union might doubt the American political commitment to Europe. (2) It is cheaper at any price to continue to support NATO now than to have to intervene in a European war later.

SELECT BIBLIOGRAPHY

Calleo, David P., "NATO's Middle Course." *Foreign Policy,* Winter 1987–88, pp. 135–47. Expert argues for a reduced U.S. role in NATO.

"NATO." *The Atlantic Community Quarterly,* Fall 1987, pp.256–342. Special section includes articles by experienced American and European government officials.

Record, Jeffrey, and Rivkin, David B., Jr., "Defending Post-INF Europe." *Foreign Affairs,* Spring 1988, pp. 735–54. Two defense experts warn that NATO faces less security in the future.

Shultz, George P., "The INF Treaty: Strengthening U.S. Security." *Department of State Bulletin,* Mar. 1988, pp. 31–39. Secretary of State reviews the negotiations and the significance of the treaty.

Sloan, Stanley R., "East-West Relations in Europe." *Headline Series* No. 278. New York, Foreign Policy Association, Mar./Apr. 1986. Problems and prospects for a divided Europe.

"Western Europe Between the Superpowers." *Great Decisions 1988.* New York, Foreign Policy Association, 1988, pp. 83–94. Overview of East-West relations in Europe since World War II.

12

South Asia: India and Pakistan

✔ *Should the U.S. favor India or Pakistan? Can the U.S. formulate policies that will satisfy both?*

✔ *Should the U.S. tie aid to Pakistan's canceling its nuclear program?*

✔ *How will an Afghan peace settlement affect U.S. policy in the region?*

The countries compared:	India	Pakistan
Population	800 mil.	105 mil.
Annual pop. growth rate	2.1%	2.9%
Armed forces	1.3 mil.	0.5 mil.
Per capita GNP	$270	$350
U.S. aid in FY 1988	$101 mil.	$611 mil.
U.S. aid FY 1946–87	$12 bil.	$9 bil.

BACKGROUND

In 1947 the British partitioned the empire they had ruled since the late 18th century into two sovereign states, India and Pakistan. Pakistan was composed mostly of Muslims; India, of Hindus. The unity of both states has been threatened since then by ethnic, religious and tribal conflicts and separatist movements.

Pakistan at independence consisted of two parts separated by northern India; in 1971 the eastern wing seceded and became Bangladesh. Differences over what constitutes an Islamic state—the goal of Pakistan's government—have long led to divisiveness.

For most of its existence Pakistan has been ruled by military strongmen, including generals Ayub Khan (1958–69), Yahya Khan (1969–71) and, since 1977, Zia ul-Haq. His presidential term expires in 1990. Zia, who instituted an Islamization program, installed a civilian prime minister, Muhammad Khan Junejo, and terminated martial law in 1985. In May 1988 Zia fired Junejo and dismissed his Cabinet and Parliament, accusing them of failing to maintain law and order and bring about an Islamic state. The constitution calls for elections within 90 days. Zia's principal opponent is Benazir Bhutto, leader of the Pakistan People's party (PPP). She is identified with the secular and socialist policies of her father, Prime Minister Zulfikar Ali Bhutto, who was deposed in 1977 and later hanged. The PPP's popularity has ebbed in the past two years.

India is the world's second most populous country and the largest democracy. It contains a multitude of ethnic and religious groups, including the world's fourth largest Muslim population. The drive for independence from Britain, led by Mahatma Gandhi, culminated in the emergence of a secular, democratic republic. The Congress party, led by members of the "Nehru dynasty," has been in power almost continuously since then. Prime Minister Jawaharlal Nehru (1947–64) was succeeded by his daughter, Indira Gandhi (1966–77 and 1980–84). After her assassination on Oct. 31, 1984, her son, Rajiv, was elected prime minister. His term expires in 1989.

Rajiv took office amid much goodwill. He called for the modernization of the country, the introduction of more competition in the economy and political reforms. Relations with the U.S. improved. However, his administration has been plagued by corruption scandals and a serious separatist movement by Sikhs, a religious minority, in the Punjab, India's richest state. Rajiv's record to date has been summed up as "good intentions, some progress, frequently weak implementation, [and] poor politics."

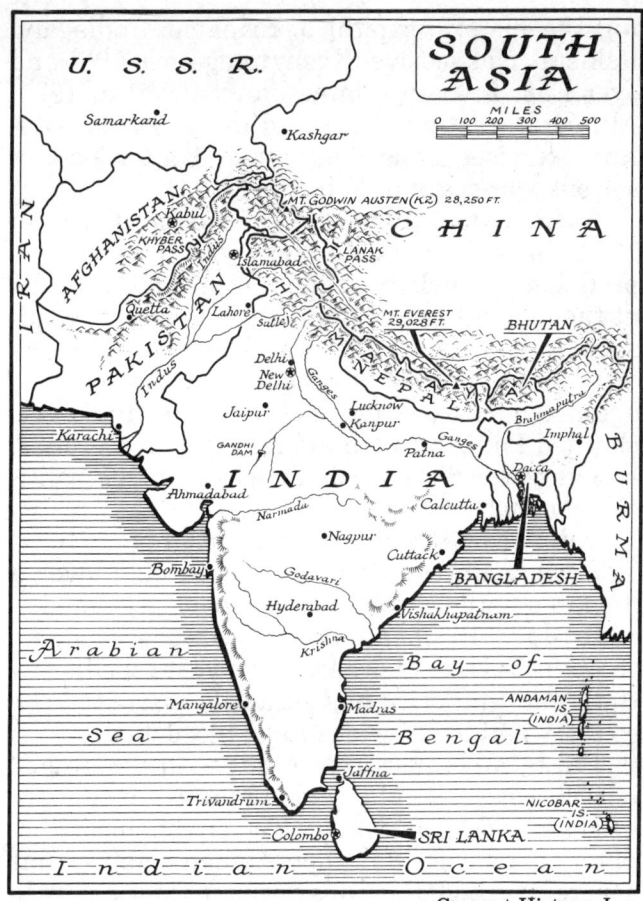

Foreign policy. Since independence India and Pakistan have fought each other in three wars. The U.S. and China have generally sided with Pakistan; the Soviet Union, with India.

A persistent bone of contention has been the northern state of Kashmir, which has a Muslim majority and joined India at independence. Pakistan objected and went to war with India. A United Nations cease-fire in 1949 divided Kashmir, with India receiving the lion's share, including the historic capital of Srinagar. India and Pakistan clashed over Kashmir again in 1965 and over East Pakistan (later Bangladesh) in 1971. Although relations improved in the 1980s, military exercises along the common border led to a serious war scare in Feb. 1987.

India (which exploded an atomic device in 1974) fears that Pakistan may soon be capable of producing a nuclear weapon. It is also disturbed at the amount of U.S. military aid going to Pakistan. India believes that Pakistan's military priority is arming for war against it, not defense against Soviet-occupied Afghanistan. India has charged Pakistan with aiding separatist groups, including the Sikhs, to weaken New Delhi's political control.

India also fears its northern neighbor, China. The two countries went to war in 1962 over a disputed border and Chinese troops prevailed.

In July 1987 India deployed peacekeeping troops in Sri Lanka, where a five-year rebellion by the Tamil minority has seriously disrupted the country and led to widespread bloodshed.

Pakistan is an insecure state with well-armed hostile powers (India and Afghanistan) on two borders, and revolutionary Iran on the third. Supplying shelter for 3 million Afghan refugees has severely taxed Pakistan's resources and goodwill.

To compensate for its military inferiority, Pakistan developed close ties with the U.S. Supporting the *mujahideen,* the insurgents fighting against the Afghan government, has enabled Pakistan to obtain substantial U.S. aid. Pakistan fears that the U.S. may abandon it once the Afghan conflict is settled.

U.S. relations with India and Pakistan. In the 1950s U.S.-Pakistani security ties were close. Pakistan was a member of the Southeast Asia Treaty Organization and the Central Treaty Organization (see Chapter 9). In 1959 the U.S. signed a bilateral security agreement with Pakistan, which it reaffirmed in 1980.

The U.S. did not support Pakistan's war against

India in 1965, but the Nixon Administration—over the objections of Congress—"tilted" toward Pakistan during its conflict with India in 1971. After the 1965 and 1971 wars, the U.S. imposed arms embargos on both sides. Pakistan, which felt the U.S. had let it down by not preventing the breakup of the country in 1971, came to view Washington as an unreliable ally. India resented the U.S. tilt toward Pakistan and relations were strained until the Carter Administration resumed development assistance in 1978.

A decade of distrust in the 1970s between Pakistan and the U.S. was replaced by close relations in the 1980s. After the fall of the shah of Iran in Jan. 1979, Pakistan became the most important U.S. friend in South Asia. The Soviet invasion of Afghanistan in Dec. 1979 transformed Pakistan into a major anti-Communist ally whose cooperation enabled the U.S. to funnel upward of $2 billion in aid to the mujahideen. In return for Pakistan's support, the U.S. initiated a six-year, $3.2 billion aid package in 1981, which included 40 F–16 fighter-bombers. In 1988—after much debate—Congress approved another $4 billion, six-year package, which could be revoked if Pakistan builds a nuclear bomb.

The Soviet role. Friendly relations between the Soviet Union and India date back to the mid-1950s, when India launched the Nonaligned Movement to oppose colonialism. Soviet economic and military assistance to India since World War II has amounted to $6 billion. In 1971 India and the Soviet Union signed a 20-year friendship treaty. India was one of the few countries that did not condemn the Soviet invasion of Afghanistan.

ADMINISTRATION POLICY

The Reagan Administration's primary goal in South Asia has been a satisfactory settlement of the Afghan conflict, for which Pakistan's cooperation is essential.

A second U.S. goal, pursued by Presidents Gerald R. Ford, Jimmy Carter and Ronald Reagan, has been to dissuade Pakistan from producing a nuclear bomb. For six years, U.S. aid to Pakistan was conditioned on the President certifying to Congress annually that Pakistan was not conducting research aimed at nuclear weapons production. In 1987, President Reagan could not give such assurances, and aid was cut off. Citing national security grounds, the President in Jan. 1988 granted Pakistan a waiver from the law until Apr. 1, 1990.

Afghan peace? On May 15, 1988, the Soviets began withdrawing their 100,000 troops from Afghanistan. They apparently decided to cut their losses in light of some 49,000 casualties (over 13,000 fatal) since 1979 in an unremitting guerrilla war with the mujahideen; an inability to foster a secure, accepted Afghan government; and widespread international condemnation, particularly by Islamic countries.

Six years of UN-sponsored negotiations between Afghanistan and Pakistan led to a peace agreement signed in Geneva on Apr. 14, 1988, that was guaranteed by both superpowers. The U.S. and Soviet Union both reserved the right to resume sending military aid to the guerrillas and the Afghan government in Kabul, respectively, but would refrain from doing so unless the other side resumed.

Still in dispute is the nature of a future Afghan government. Pakistan favors the formation of a coalition, with power shared by the resistance leaders, Afghan exiles, and Communists associated with the Soviet-backed regime of President Najibullah. Pakistan fears that if Najibullah is left in power, civil strife will continue and the refugees from Afghanistan will not return home. The alliance of seven Afghan resistance leaders, dominated by Islamic fundamentalists and based in Pakistan, has denounced the Geneva accords.

India. U.S. relations with India have warmed somewhat since the accession of Rajiv Gandhi. At their meeting in Washington, D.C., in Oct. 1987, President Reagan assured Gandhi that the U.S. objective in South Asia was stability and reduced tensions, and that U.S. aid to Pakistan was not directed against India.

Since 1984, the U.S. has sought closer defense and technological ties with India. In 1986 the U.S. gave India permission to purchase an advanced jet engine for light combat aircraft and in 1987 the U.S. agreed to sell India a coveted supercomputer for use in weather forecasting. (The U.S. had long feared that India would leak secrets to the Soviet Union.)

Most U.S. support for India is currently channelled through the World Bank, to which the U.S. is the largest contributor. India is unhappy with the low level of direct aid for economic development ($24 million in fiscal year 1988).

POLICY CHOICES

❐ The U.S. should tilt toward India, not Pakistan.
Yes. (1) India, unlike Pakistan, is a democracy and shares many American values. (2) India is the most powerful country in the subcontinent and the largest market for U.S. goods.
No. (1) Pakistan is pro-American and supports U.S. policy goals; India does not. (2) Pakistan is a useful bridge to other Islamic countries, particularly Iran and the Arab Gulf states.

❐ The U.S. should withhold aid to Pakistan until it suspends nuclear weapons development.
Yes. (1) Making an exception for Pakistan undermines U.S. antiproliferation efforts. (2) Pakistani nuclear research exacerbates regional tensions and could lead to another war with India.
No. (1) Pakistani gratitude for U.S. aid has deterred it from testing a nuclear device. (2) If the U.S. provides adequate conventional arms, Pakistan will not feel the need to develop nuclear weapons.

SELECT BIBLIOGRAPHY

"Afghanistan: Eight Years of Soviet Occupation." *Department of State Bulletin,* Mar. 1988, pp. 1–24. Thorough annual assessment of the war.

Bouton, Marshall M., ed., *India Briefing, 1988.* Boulder, Colo., Westview Press for The Asia Society, 1988. Overview of major developments in India in 1987.

Kreisberg, Paul H., "Gandhi at Midterm." *Foreign Affairs,* Summer 1987, pp. 1055–76. Gandhi must become a more effective politician in order to solve India's problems.

"Pakistan Survey." *The Economist* (London), Jan. 17, 1987. Excellent profile of Pakistan.

Smith, Hedrick, "A Bomb Ticks in Pakistan." *The New York Times Magazine,* Mar. 6, 1988. U.S. dilemmas in dealing with a nuclear-armed Pakistan.

13

Gorbachev's Soviet Union

✔ *How much are Soviet policies changing?*

✔ *How should the U.S. respond to these changes?*

✔ *Is greater cooperation with the Soviet Union possible? Is it desirable?*

BACKGROUND

The U.S. did not establish diplomatic relations with the Soviet Union until 1933, 16 years after the Bolsheviks had seized power in the October Revolution. Relations between the two countries were strained by the U.S. sending troops to support anti-Bolshevik forces during the 1918–19 civil war, by Moscow's attempts to export revolution to Europe in the 1920s and by the U.S.S.R.'s unwillingness to pay czarist debts.

World War II temporarily united the two countries against a common enemy, Germany's Adolf Hitler. The cold war started soon after the Allied victory, however, when the Soviet Union began taking control of its East European neighbors by manipulating elections and stifling dissent. By 1948, Poland, Czechoslovakia, Hungary, Romania, Bulgaria and Albania were under Soviet hegemony. The U.S. responded in 1949 by forming the North Atlantic Treaty Organization (NATO) to protect Western Europe and "contain" communism.

Superpower relations. Each of the U.S.S.R.'s leaders since then has left his mark on the super-

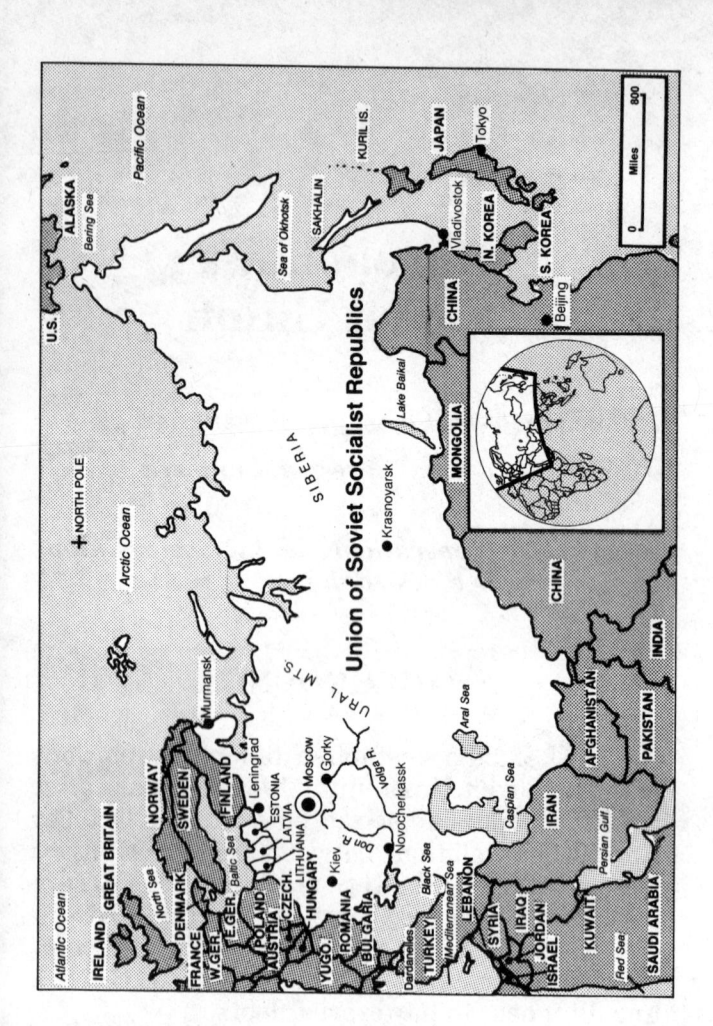

Country statistics

Population (mid-1988 est.):
286 million

Area:
8.7 million sq. mi.

GNP (1985 est.):
$2.2 trillion

Rate of GNP growth (1987 est.):
0.5% *

Defense spending (1987 est.):
15%–17% of GNP *

* Joint Economic Committee of Congress

power relationship. Joseph Stalin built the Iron Curtain and retreated into hostile isolation behind it. Superpower tensions were heightened by Moscow's blockade of Berlin (1948–50) and by the Korean War (1950–53). Nikita S. Khrushchev made the Soviet Union an active player in world affairs, involving Moscow in Third World political struggles and bringing the superpowers to the brink of nuclear war when he placed Soviet missiles in Cuba (1962). Leonid I. Brezhnev transformed the U.S.S.R. into a nuclear superpower in the 1960s and worked with the U.S. to forge *détente,* a lessening of tensions, by seeking agreements in areas of mutual interest, such as arms control and trade. The Moscow summit conference of 1972 marked the zenith of détente. Brezhnev and President Richard M. Nixon signed the SALT I (strategic arms limitation talks) agreements limiting deployment of antiballistic missile systems (the ABM treaty) and placing ceilings on strategic nuclear ballistic missile launchers. Both leaders agreed not to seek "unilateral advantage," said they would "exercise restraint" in mutual relations, and initialed trade and scientific cooperation accords. At the 35-nation Conference on Security and Cooperation in Europe in Helsinki, Finland, in 1975, the West accepted postwar boundaries in Europe, including the division of Germany, in return for Soviet promises to permit a freer exchange of ideas and people between East and West.

Détente foundered on the divergent U.S. and Soviet views on the arms race, Soviet policies in the Third World and on human rights. Brezhnev and President Jimmy Carter did sign a second arms limitation agreement (SALT II) in 1979, but the Senate never ratified the treaty (although both governments agreed to honor its terms).

Reagan and Gorbachev. Polemics between the superpowers were more strident during the first four years of Ronald Reagan's presidency than they had been since the Cuban missile crisis. Reagan's first term coincided with a succession crisis in the U.S.S.R. The death of Brezhnev in 1982 was followed by the demise of his successors Yuri V. Andropov (68) in Feb. 1984 and Konstantin U. Chernenko (73) in Mar. 1985. Meanwhile, the U.S. engaged in a major military buildup (see Chapter 3) and progress on arms control stalled.

Since the accession of Mikhail S. Gorbachev to leadership, the atmosphere has improved. There have been four summit meetings, and agreements on a variety of topics have been signed, including the Dec. 1987 intermediate-range nuclear forces (INF) treaty that eliminates an entire class of nuclear weapons.

Gorbachev's reforms. Gorbachev inherited a country in trouble, domestically and internationally. Economic growth had slowed dramatically since the 1960s. Productivity, especially in agriculture, was low; energy sources and other needed raw materials were scarcer; industrial machinery and equipment were aging. Social ills—alcoholism, divorce, corruption and infant mortality—were all on the rise. Internationally, after reaching a pinnacle of military and diplomatic power in the late 1970s, the Soviet Union suffered reversals in countries where it had invested heavily.

Gorbachev launched a variety of domestic and foreign policy initiatives to reverse the country's sagging fortunes. American observers are divided as to how substantial these changes are and how the U.S. should react.

Domestic reforms. Under Gorbachev's policy of *glasnost,* meaning openness, or public airing, the Soviet press today runs stories on social ills and government corruption that were previously taboo. Formerly banned books, films and plays have been released. Some increased emigration has been permitted, and political prisoners have been freed. Gorbachev has cracked down on alcoholism and absenteeism in the workplace, and has begun an ambitious policy of restructuring *(perestroika)* that he hopes will increase economic

The dashing new jockey, Gorbachev, and his sleek thoroughbred

By Payne for Scripps Howard.

efficiency. Measures include applications of some free-market concepts: giving individual enterprises more autonomy within the centrally managed economy; making wage increases and bonuses dependent on a business showing a profit, rather than meeting a numerical quota; and legalizing some small-scale private enterprise. Gorbachev has also removed some of the many administrative blocks to foreign trade in an attempt to open new markets to Soviet goods and to gain greater access to Western expertise and technology.

Gorbachev has encountered political opposition to his programs, and many believe he has had to proceed more slowly than he would like. Although economic indicators improved after his first year in office, most Western analysts think that the fundamental contradiction inherent in trying market reforms in a centrally planned economy will prevent the U.S.S.R. from achieving the goals Gorbachev has set.

Foreign policy. Gorbachev's personal dynamism and his reform program have given him a favorable public image in the West. He has made new diplomatic approaches to China, Japan, Israel, conservative Arab states and a wider variety of Third World countries than Moscow has dealt with in the past, and has supported a strengthening of the role of the United Nations. He has been eager for arms control talks and has agreed to provisions for the verification of compliance with signed agreements—such as on-site inspections in the Soviet Union—that few American arms control experts would have thought possible just a few years ago. Analysts disagree over his long-term motives but agree that in the short run Gorbachev is seeking a "breathing space" in U.S.-Soviet relations to give his economic reforms a chance to work.

The military. Gorbachev has maintained the traditional Soviet commitment to a strong military. Soviet defense spending has picked up slightly since Gorbachev took power, growing at roughly 3% in 1986 compared with 2% per year between 1975 and 1985. The Administration is concerned by the increasing size and quality of the Soviet navy and air force in the Pacific. Although U.S. analysts doubt that the Soviet fleet would be a match for the U.S. Navy in a war, they believe the buildup can give the Soviet Union greater political weight in the region.

Eastern Europe. Gorbachev has also made clear his continued commitment to preserving Moscow's empire in Eastern Europe. Here, too, Gorbachev has demonstrated more flexibility than past leaders, encouraging East European governments to be creative in addressing economic problems.

ADMINISTRATION POLICY

The Reagan Administration has proceeded on the assumption that the best way for the U.S. to forge a constructive relationship with its chief global competitor is to negotiate from a position of military strength. It points to Moscow's return to the arms control table as evidence that the policy has succeeded. The Administration has pursued a four-part agenda with the Soviet leadership: human rights, arms control (see Chapter 2), regional conflicts and bilateral issues. It has not, however, linked progress in one area to progress in another but has pursued each independently.

Human rights. While welcoming some movement on human rights, including the release of well-known dissidents, increases in Soviet Jewish emigration and the easing of some restrictions on freedom of expression, Washington emphasizes that changes so far have been modest. Gorbachev, in turn, has accused the U.S. of "organizing...a brain drain" to the West by its support for the right of dissidents to emigrate. Moscow continues to refuse people permission to leave on the grounds that they are privy to "state secrets."

Regional conflicts. *Afghanistan:* In May 1988, after an eight-and-a-half year war that Gorbachev called a "bleeding wound," the Soviet Union began pulling out its 100,000 troops from Afghanistan. Under a UN-sponsored accord, signed in Apr. by the U.S., U.S.S.R., Afghanistan and Pakistan, the U.S. and Soviet Union agreed to stop supplying the rebels and the government, respectively, with military aid unless the other continued to do so. *Angola:* See Chapter 10. *Central America:* Although Gorbachev hinted at the Dec. 1987 summit that the Soviet Union might cut off its aid to Nicaragua's Sandinista government, Moscow's assistance has actually been increasing. The Reagan Administration has warned that it would not accept the basing of Soviet aircraft in Nicaragua. *Middle East:* See Chapter 9.

Bilateral relations. Since the 1985 Geneva summit, the Reagan Administration has worked out agreements with the Soviet Union on academic, cultural, scientific and people-to-people exchanges. A scientific cooperation accord, signed in early 1988, brings U.S.-Soviet cooperation to the highest level since the Soviet invasion of Afghanistan in Dec. 1979. The agreement paves the way for joint research on earthquake prediction, AIDS, the depletion of the ozone layer and nuclear reactor safety.

U.S.-Soviet trade, though limited, has increased somewhat, and the Soviet Union is eager for further expansion. But U.S. restrictions are linked by legislation to Soviet improvements on emigration issues. The Jackson-Vanik and Stevenson amendments to the Trade Act of 1974 tied most-favored-nation treatment and credits for Soviet exports to a relaxation of Soviet restrictions on Jewish emigration. Congress has not moved to repeal or amend these provisions.

POLICY CHOICES

☐ The U.S. should pursue warmer relations with the Soviet Union.
Yes. (1) Gorbachev's reforms have signaled a fundamental change in Soviet policy and offer an opportunity for a more constructive, less confrontational superpower relationship. (2) If his economic reforms succeed, they may pave the way for political liberalization and make the Soviet Union a less dangerous world power.
No. (1) The U.S. should condition improved relations on real changes of direction by Moscow, e.g., removal of the Berlin Wall and withdrawal from Eastern Europe. (2) To loosen trade restrictions, provide cheap loans, and otherwise help the U.S.S.R. put its house in order is to help subsidize the eventual reemergence of a more dangerous adversary.

☐ The U.S. should link trade and arms control concessions to Soviet economic reforms, military spending cuts and human rights improvements.
Yes. If the U.S. wants to see progress on human rights and other issues, it will have to structure a package deal that offers Moscow something significant in return, namely trade, credits and arms agreements.

No. U.S. leverage on Moscow is limited. Moreover, stability in the superpower relationship is too central to security in the nuclear age to hold increased cooperation hostage to issues, such as human rights, that are unlikely to be resolved soon.

SELECT BIBLIOGRAPHY

Gorbachev, Mikhail, *Perestroika: New Thinking for Our Country and the World.* New York, Harper & Row, 1987. Soviet leader's ideas for restructuring Soviet society and foreign policy.

Legvold, Robert, and The Task Force on Soviet New Thinking, "Gorbachev's Foreign Policy: How Should the United States Respond?" *Headline Series* No. 284. New York, Foreign Policy Association, Apr. 1988. Analysis of what has changed.

Reagan, Ronald, "The Agenda of U.S.-Soviet Relations." *Department of State Bulletin.* Dec. 1987, pp. 5–7. Text of an Oct. 1987 address.

"The Soviet Union: Gorbachev's Reforms." *Great Decisions 1988.* New York, Foreign Policy Association, 1988, pp. 37–48. Overview of Gorbachev's domestic and foreign policies.

14
Canada: A Good Neighbor

✔ *Is free trade with Canada good for the U.S.?*

✔ *Does the U.S. have a responsibility to curb acid rain?*

✔ *Does Canada contribute enough to NATO?*

BACKGROUND

The U.S. and Canada, the world's two largest trading partners, share a 5,000-mile border—the longest unfortified frontier in the world. They also share similar cultures and security interests. By and large their relationship is very good.

The election of Prime Minister Brian Mulroney's Progressive Conservative government in 1984 signaled the end of a period of friction between the previous Liberal government of Pierre Elliot Trudeau and the Reagan Administration. Since the first summit between Mulroney and President Ronald Reagan in Ottawa, Canada's capital, in 1985, the two leaders have met yearly. Their major achievement is the free trade agreement of Jan. 1988, which must be approved by the Canadian Parliament and the U.S. Congress.

Trade. Canada is the most open and growing market for the U.S. In 1987, U.S.-Canadian trade in goods and services was worth $163 billion. Major U.S. exports to Canada are automobiles, auto parts, and computers; major U.S. imports from Canada are automobiles and parts, oil and natural gas, and wood products. After exporting to Canada more than it had imported every year

The countries compared:	Canada	U.S.
Real GNP (1987)	$404 billion	$4.50 trillion
Per capita GNP	$15,595	$18,411
GNP growth rate (1987)	3.7%	3.8%
Defense spending as % of GNP	2.0%	6.5%
Exports to U.S/Canada as % of total exports	73%	24%
Foreign direct investment in U.S./Canada	$18.3 billion	$60.3 billion
Population	25.9 million	244 million
Unemployment	7.7%	5.4%

since 1946, the U.S. began running a merchandise trade deficit with Canada in 1980. In 1987 this deficit was $13 billion but was offset by a favorable balance in services and capital flows.

Canada's economy, one tenth as large as that of the U.S., is dependent on the U.S. market, which absorbs almost three quarters of its exports. Canada is therefore greatly influenced by U.S. policies and behavior. Canadian "nationalists" fear the effect of this influence on their economy and culture and tend to favor protectionist trade measures; "internationalists" favor the free flow of ideas and dollars across the border.

Investment. One third of all U.S. foreign direct investment is in Canada. To encourage a continued flow of investment from the U.S. and other sources, Prime Minister Mulroney, an internationalist, in 1985 eliminated the restrictive Foreign Investment Review Agency and replaced it with the Investment Canada Act. As a result, U.S. investment has increased, although it is still heavily regulated in comparison with Canadian investment in the U.S.

1988 free trade agreement (FTA). Canada's increasing dependence on the U.S. market for its exports at a time of rising protectionism in the U.S. Congress prompted Mulroney to propose discussion of a free trade agreement in 1985. Twenty years earlier, the two countries had eliminated tariffs on automobiles and auto parts, but Canadian goods still faced U.S. quotas and other nontariff barriers, and 30% of U.S. exports were subject to Canadian tariffs. Although the negotiations threatened to founder on more than one occasion, Mulroney and Reagan signed the FTA on Jan. 2, 1988. If the agreement is approved (Congress, under the "fast track" negotiating authority, can either accept or reject it, but cannot amend it), it will create an increasingly open market for bilateral trade and investment.

The agreement, which would go into effect Jan. 1, 1989, provides for:

• elimination of all tariffs and nontariff barriers to bilateral trade by 1998;

• increased investment rights and the establishment of rules for the conduct of bilateral investment;

• revisions to the 1965 automobile agreement;

• a dispute settlement mechanism;

• elimination of government restrictions on energy trade; and

• liberalization of trade in services (e.g., banking, insurance, telecommunications, data processing). This is the first international trade agreement ever to deal with services in a comprehensive way.

The agreement will not cover "cultural industries," such as film, recording, publishing and broadcasting.

Advocates for the agreement in both countries see it as a catalyst for multilateral trade talks—proof that it is still possible to solve trade differences through negotiations. They say it will stimulate economic growth, lower prices, and expand employment opportunities. But nationalists in Canada say they are "willing to pay higher prices not to become Americans." In the U.S., while many high-technology, service and manufacturing industries stand to gain from lower tariffs, there is opposition from farmers, some unions and the shipping, textile and natural resource (e.g. uranium and plywood) industries.

Acid rain. A major sore point between the U.S. and Canada is acid rain, which is created by emissions of sulfur dioxide (formed primarily in the process of generating power from coal and from ore-refining processes) and nitrogen oxides (formed mainly in fuel combustion). These compounds are carried in the atmosphere by prevailing winds and returned to earth in the form of rain, snow, fog or dust. Acid rain has been identified as a serious threat to the environment since the early 1960s, and U.S.-Canadian examination of the issue has been under way since 1978. Canada wants the U.S. to limit the flow of pollutants across the border to eastern Canada, which receives higher than acceptable levels of acid rain.

U.S. emissions are regulated by the 1970 Clean Air Act, and individual states are responsible for making sure that emissions within their borders conform to its standards. Compliance with the Clean Air Act costs U.S. industries about $25 billion annually, and their representatives in Congress have consistently opposed legislation that would add to the expense.

In 1985, Canadian provincial environment ministers agreed to lower 1980 sulfur dioxide emission levels by 50% by 1994. The Canadian program will cost roughly $375 million annually over 20 years. The same year, Reagan and Mulroney each appointed a personal special envoy to examine the situation and to make recommendations. Their resulting joint report called for a five-year, $5 billion U.S. program that would test new emission-control options. At the same time, it would bring about some near-term reductions in

U.S. emissions affecting Canada, without initially committing a great deal of money to the project. Only half of the funding committed by the U.S. in accordance with the plan has so far been allocated to acid rain research.

After their 1987 meeting, Mulroney expected that Reagan would act to reduce transborder pollution. The U.S. insists it never made such a pledge; that it considered the problem, as promised, but rejected the treaty Canada proposed.

Defense. Canada is the front line of North American defense; all nuclear missiles and bombers launched from Soviet territory would have to pass over Canadian territory to reach the U.S. Canada is therefore a critical location for early-warning radars and other detection systems. Canada has been a member of the North Atlantic Treaty Organization (NATO) since the alliance was founded in 1949, and has also been a member of the North American Aerospace Defense Command (NORAD) since 1958.

One bone of contention between the U.S. and Canada has been Canada's consistently small contribution to NATO. Mulroney agreed with Reagan at the 1985 summit to contribute some 12% of the $7 billion needed to overhaul the aging NORAD detection systems. A 1987 White Paper on Canadian defense policy committed Canada to defense increases of just over 3% annually for the next 15 years. The White Paper also called for 10–12 new nuclear-powered submarines that can operate under Arctic ice and provide for three-ocean defense.

Only a minority of critics believe that Canada should pull out of NORAD and NATO and demilitarize the Arctic Circle. But many Canadians of all political stripes have serious reservations about nuclear weapons and about expanding the armed forces, and they fear that defense modernization may eventually lead to the stationing of nuclear weapons on their territory, despite assurances by the Mulroney government that it will not.

Northwest Passage. The status of the Northwest Passage remains a point of dispute between Ottawa and Washington. Canada claims sovereignty over this body of water, while the U.S. considers it an international strait. When the U.S. Coast Guard icebreaker *Polar Sea* went through the Northwest Passage in Aug. 1985, it brought the issue to a head. Negotiations began in the fall of 1985, and observers expect an agreement that will permit the U.S. the access it wants without violating Canada's concerns for its sovereignty. Canada is also planning to spend $450 million for a Polar Class icebreaker to help patrol the territory as part of its defense modernization program.

ADMINISTRATION POLICY

Trade. The Reagan Administration strongly supports the FTA and hopes it will be a catalyst for multilateral trade negotiations.

Acid rain. Before taking further action, the Administration believes that more research is needed to determine the extent of damage actually caused by acid rain and whether it justifies the huge expense of controlling emissions. Progress has been stalled by conflicting study results.

Defense and sovereignty. The Administration welcomes the Mulroney government's pledge to increase defense spending. Despite reservations among some U.S. military officials about Canada's plans to build a fleet of nuclear-powered submarines, Reagan in Apr. 1988 approved Canada's plan to purchase submarines that use American nuclear technology.

POLICY CHOICES

❐ The U.S. should wholeheartedly support freer trade with Canada.
Yes. (1) The agreement will promote U.S. exports and investment in Canada, the largest U.S. trad-

ing partner, and should enhance U.S. energy security. (2) The success of the U.S.-Canadian deal will give impetus to multilateral trade negotiations currently under way, and should help ward off the increasing dangers of rising protectionism to the world economy.
No. (1) There is no assurance that the next Canadian administration will stand by the FTA. (2) The natural resource, textile and shipping industries could suffer; as a saying on Capitol Hill goes, "Winners are everyone east of the Mississippi and California; losers are the rest of the country."

❐ The U.S. should curb the flow of emissions responsible for acid rain across the Canadian border.
Yes. (1) Acid rain is damaging the U.S. as well as the Canadian environment. (2) U.S. failure to keep its promise has soured U.S. relations with its major trade partner.
No. (1) It is still not known how serious the effects of acid rain are, and reducing it is expensive. (2) The U.S. is living up to its obligations by studying the problem and has already committed substantial funds to the issue.

SELECT BIBLIOGRAPHY

"Canada." *Current History,* Mar. 1988. Entire issue devoted to Canadian policies and problems.

Diebold, William, Jr., ed., *Bilateralism, Multilateralism and Canada in U.S. Trade Policy.* Cambridge, Mass., Ballinger Publishing Co. for the Council on Foreign Relations, 1988. Background and implications of the FTA.

Reagan, Ronald, "U.S., Canada Sign Free Trade Agreement." *Department of State Bulletin,* Mar. 1988, p. 58. President's Jan. 2, 1988, statement, followed by White House fact sheet on the FTA.

15

Mexico in Transition

✔ *What steps can help ease Mexico's debt crisis?*
✔ *Should the U.S. close the door to Mexican immigrants?*
✔ *Is Mexico doing enough to stem drug traffic?*

The countries compared:	Mexico	U.S.
Population (1987)	83 mil.	244 mil.
GNP per capita (1987)	$1,900	$18,411
GNP growth rate (1987)	1%	3.8%
Foreign debt	$105 bil.	$400 bil.
Exports to the other (1987)	$20.5 bil.	$14.6 bil.

FACTS

- Mexico is the third largest U.S. trade partner and its largest foreign supplier of oil.
- Mexico owes one fourth of its foreign debt of $105 billion to U.S. banks.
- Mexico is suffering from low growth (1% in 1987) and high inflation (150%); real wages have declined 50% over the past five years; unemployment is high.
- One third of the marijuana, heroin and cocaine entering the U.S. comes via Mexico.
- Mexico and the U.S. will both elect new presidents in 1988.

BACKGROUND

Mexico and the U.S. share a 2,000-mile border and are extensively linked by family, economic and cultural ties. Some 12 million Americans are of Mexican descent. The countries' economies are interdependent: many U.S. employers rely on Mexican labor; Mexicans, faced with widespread unemployment, rely on jobs in the U.S. Some 3,900 U.S.-owned companies operate in Mexico.

Mexico profile. The Institutional Revolutionary party (PRI) has been in power since 1929. The PRI has provided remarkable political stability and, for three decades following World War II, rapid economic growth. Large oil discoveries in the 1970s led to greatly increased state income and huge expenditures on the government-controlled oil industry. The boom ended in 1981 when demand for oil dropped due to the world recession. By Aug. 1982 Mexico could no longer pay the interest on its debt of $85 billion.

The debt crisis. In 1982 Mexico negotiated an austerity program with the International Monetary Fund (IMF) requiring a cut in imports, the sale of unprofitable government-owned enterprises and a reduction in subsidies for consumer goods. For a time, Mexico was considered a model debtor. Imposing economic discipline and improving its balance of payments, however, came at the expense of domestic growth and caused great hardship to poor Mexicans. By 1986, Mexico faced its worst financial crisis in half a century due to another decline in oil prices, abandonment of the austerity plan and a drop in demand for Mexican products. The economic situation improved in 1987 due to higher oil prices, foreign loans and the repatriation of capital. Mexico seemed on the road to recovery. However, the Wall Street crash of Oct. 1987 severely shook confidence, and led to fears that exports to the U.S., crucial for economic recovery, would shrink.

Political uncertainty. This economic setback came at a time of political transition. Mexico is an anomaly in Latin America—it is nominally a democracy but its government is more authoritarian than most in the region. Many Mexicans believe that the PRI's primary concern is to perpetuate its rule. President Miguel de la Madrid Hurtado, who must step down when his six-year term expires in Dec. 1988, is credited with improving government accountability and introducing discipline into the economy. However, his unexpected devaluation of the peso in the wake of the Wall Street crash, after promises that he would maintain economic stability, hurt his credibility. It will make it more difficult for Carlos Salinas de Gortari, the PRI's candidate for president in the July 1988 election, to restore discipline.

Legacy of distrust. Mexico lost one half of its territory to the U.S. in the mid-19th century and is sensitive about U.S. intervention in its affairs. Relations since World War II have been cordial, although there was some tension in the late 1970s when Mexico supported Third World demands for a greater voice in the international economic system and supported the Sandinista government in Nicaragua. In 1985 and 1986, relations reached a low point due to mutual recriminations over the control of drug trafficking.

Many Mexicans believe the U.S. tends to be patronizing and should accord Mexico a higher priority in its foreign affairs. They believe the image U.S. citizens hold of their country is out of date. The U.S. has traditionally taken Mexico for granted and has criticized Mexicans for not taking stronger medicine to cure their problems.

The two countries' outstanding differences include policy on:

■ **Immigration**. Much Mexican emigration to the U.S. in pursuit of jobs has been temporary and unregulated. A major exception was the Bracero Program, which lured Mexicans to the U.S. to fill jobs left vacant during World War II. The program was considered successful by growers (although opposed by U.S. labor unions), and continued until 1964. By 1986 an estimated 1 million Mexicans each year were entering the U.S. illegally. Many U.S. employers depend on these illegal aliens (also referred to as undocumented workers) for low-paid, often seasonal labor. Mexico depends on the "safety valve" that U.S. jobs provide and on the remittances these workers send their families.

The Immigration Reform and Control Act, which took effect in Nov. 1986, is intended to stop illegal immigration, while permitting immigrants who had come here before 1982 to stay. It imposes sanctions on employers who hire illegal aliens. (In the past only the employee was penalized.) Of an estimated 3.9 million aliens eligible for amnesty, 1.6 million applied before the cutoff date of May 4, 1988. A provision in the law that allows seasonal farm workers to gain permanent residence in the U.S. attracted an additional 500,000 applicants.

■ **The debt crisis.** The U.S. and Mexico agree that economic growth is the only long-term solution to the debt crisis, and that this growth cannot take place unless Mexico receives relief in paying off its debts. They disagree as to how the responsibility for relieving the burden should be apportioned among Mexico, the U.S. government and U.S. banks. The U.S. government and bankers maintained until recently that all the debt had to be repaid. (Mexico's debt service in 1988 amounts to $10 billion.) The Baker Plan of Oct. 1985 called for greatly increased bank lending to Mexico and other Latin American debtors if they adopted free-market policies. However, this lending did not occur.

In 1987, U.S. bankers acknowledged that full repayment was unlikely. Major lenders set aside reserves ($3 billion in the case of Citibank) to cover anticipated losses. The Bank of Boston wrote off $200 million in loans to developing countries. In Dec., J.P. Morgan and Co. proposed a method of relief that was well received by some bankers and the U.S. and Mexican governments. It calls on banks to forgive billions of dollars in Mexican debt in return for bonds issued by Mexico that are backed by zero-coupon U.S. Treasury bonds. Since they do not pay interest until they mature in 20 years, Mexico could buy the Treasury bonds for about a fifth of their face value. The plan was more attractive to the smaller banks than to those holding the largest debt (with the most to lose) such as Citibank. The high expectations raised by the plan were dashed when an auction for the bonds in Mar. 1988 brought disappointing results. Banks received about 70 cents on the dollar for their loans. Mexico was only able to reduce its debt by $1.1 billion.

Other Latin American countries mired in debt, such as Brazil ($110 billion) and Argentina ($54 billion), were discouraged from following the Morgan plan. Debt and high inflation, as in Mexico, have stalled growth and imperiled their recent return to democracy.

■ **Trade.** In 1987, U.S.-Mexican trade amounted to $35 billion. The U.S. is the largest supplier and largest market for Mexico; Mexico is the third largest customer of the U.S. and the fifth largest supplier.

In the past the U.S. has urged Mexico to lift the protectionist barriers it put in place after World War II, with the eventual goal of creating a free-trade zone linking it with the U.S. and Canada. Recently, significant trade liberalization has occurred. In July 1986, Mexico joined the General Agreement on Tariffs and Trade (GATT), which will result in increased exports and will expose the domestic market to foreign competition. In Oct. 1987 the U.S. and Mexico signed a trade pact. They agreed on a mechanism to settle trade disputes as well as a framework to liberalize trade in textiles and steel—the two most important exports to the U.S. after oil—and other products.

After oil, Mexico's largest source of foreign exchange are the 1,400 *maquiladora* industries located along the U.S.-Mexican border. These companies, primarily U.S.-owned, import materials from the U.S. and ship finished products back to the U.S., which levies a tax only on the value added by the goods' assembly. Maquiladoras are opposed by American labor unions which charge that U.S. companies are moving thousands of jobs to Mexico (where the going wage is 60 cents an hour).

■ **Drug trafficking.** Mexico contends a large part of the drug problem is U.S. demand. Mexico in 1987 spent $21.5 million on drug-eradication efforts; the U.S. chipped in an additional $14.5 million. PRI-nominee Salinas says that the production and transportation of drugs are greater problems for Mexico than for the U.S. because they undermine national security. Tensions were strained in Jan. 1988 when the U.S. implicated senior Mexican army officials in a plot to smuggle cocaine to the U.S. The State Department reported on Mar. 1, 1988, that drug production in Mexico rose in 1987, and criticized Mexico for not doing more to control drug trafficking. Nevertheless, President Reagan certified to Congress that

Mexico was cooperating with the U.S. In spite of this, the Senate voted to impose sanctions, which the President can waive (see Chapter 7).

■ **Central America.** Mexico does not share the Reagan Administration's fear of Communist subversion in this hemisphere. It believes political upheaval results from social and economic inequities in the region. Mexico has supported the Sandinista government in Nicaragua, but relations cooled under de la Madrid. Mexico spearheaded efforts toward a regional peace settlement by joining with Colombia, Venezuela and Panama to form the Contadora Group in Jan. 1983. Salinas also has strongly backed the Guatemala peace plan (see Chapter 8).

ADMINISTRATION POLICY

The Administration has supported de la Madrid's austerity program and is pleased that Salinas is committed to carrying it on. Differences over the debt problem have narrowed, and by endorsing the Morgan plan, the Administration

By Signe Wilkinson, *Philadelphia Daily News.*

"OK, YOU HUDDLED MASSES. I KNOW YOU'RE IN HERE."

has shown a new willingness to contribute to a solution.

The Administration has clashed with Mexico over how to combat the international drug traffic and complains that Mexico is not doing enough.

Regarding trade relations, the U.S. sees the 1987 trade pact as a step toward facilitating freer trade. The agreement does not provide for binding arbitration, as does the trade pact with Canada. At the Feb. 1988 Mazatlán summit, the U.S. agreed to allow Mexican textiles increased access to U.S. markets.

On immigration, the U.S. is monitoring the effects of the new law and may propose some amendments.

The Administration has been unenthusiastic about the Contadora initiative and the Guatemala peace plan.

POLICY CHOICES

❏ The U.S. should accord relations with Mexico a higher priority.
Yes. (1) The U.S. cannot take Mexico for granted. Since the two countries' economies are interdependent, social or political instability in Mexico can affect the U.S. (2) It is in the U.S. interest to deal with Mexican problems before they become U.S. problems.
No. (1) The two countries do cooperate on a broad range of issues and, for the most part, relations are amicable. (2) As a world power, the U.S. has many foreign policy concerns and some, such as arms control and U.S.-Soviet relations, are higher on the list than Mexico.

❏ The U.S. should make it easier for Mexican workers to enter the U.S. for temporary periods.
Yes. (1) U.S. employers depend on Mexican workers and it lowers costs to American consumers. (2) If unemployed Mexicans are denied entrance, political instability in Mexico will increase.

No. (1) Cheap Mexican labor denies jobs to Americans and strains social services. (2) Mexico should reform its economy and not count on exporting its unemployment to the U.S.

☐ The U.S. government should take the lead in resolving the debt crisis.
Yes. (1) Mexico is doing all it can to repay the debt, even though its government could suffer adverse political consequences. (2) If the U.S. government is serious about solving the debt problem, it must contribute money, not just rhetoric.
No. (1) Mexico bears the prime responsibility for its debt and, together with its creditors, must work out a solution. (2) It is unfair for Mexico and the banks to expect the U.S. government to bail them out.

SELECT BIBLIOGRAPHY

"Mexico Survey." *The Economist* (London), Sept. 5, 1987. Incisive profile of Mexico today.

"President's Visit to Mexico." *Department of State Bulletin,* May 1988, p. 6. Text of joint remarks.

Purcell, Susan Kaufman, ed., *Mexico in Transition: Implications for U.S. Policy.* New York, Council on Foreign Relations, 1988. Essays from both sides of the border.

Riding, Alan, *Distant Neighbors: A Portrait of the Mexicans.* New York, Vintage Books, 1986. Widely acclaimed portrait of the Mexicans by *New York Times* correspondent.

Smith, Peter H., "Mexico: Neighbor in Transition." *Headline Series* No. 267. New York, Foreign Policy Association, Jan./Feb. 1984. Mexico faces a long-term process of political and social transformation that could have enormous consequences for the U.S.

16

China and Taiwan

✔ *Is it in the U.S. interest to strengthen China economically and militarily?*

✔ *Should the U.S. continue to sell arms to Taiwan?*

✔ *How can the U.S. reduce its trade deficit with Taiwan?*

The countries compared:	China	Taiwan
Population	1.1 bil.	20 mil.
Gross national product per capita (1985)	$310	$3,250
Merchandise exports (1985)	$27.3 bil.	$30.7 bil.
GNP real growth (1985)	12.3%	5.1%
Trade with U.S. (1985)	10.9%	38.4%
Debt (1986)	$25–$27 bil.	$8 bil.

BACKGROUND

The People's Republic of China (PRC) was founded in 1949 following the Communist victory in the civil war with Nationalist forces. The Nationalists fled to the island province of Taiwan, 80 miles offshore, and established the Republic of China (ROC). Each party claimed it was the sole legal government of China.

The Chinese Communist party, led by Mao

Zedong, established control over the mainland, rebuilt the economy and strengthened the military. China initially welcomed Soviet aid and advisers, but began to split with the Soviets in the late 1950s. It instituted the disastrous Great Leap Forward in 1958, a program aimed at raising industrial and agricultural production. From 1966–76 China was convulsed by the Cultural Revolution, a period of anarchy in which radical youth groups known as Red Guards rooted out officials believed sympathetic to capitalism.

China's policies moderated after the death of Mao in 1976. Vice Premier Deng Xiaoping, who took control in 1977, introduced a series of reforms intended to modernize the country while not abandoning the basic principles of socialism, dictatorship of the proletariat, Communist party leadership and Marxism-Leninism-Mao Zedong thought. The reforms include decentralizing power within the party and replacing aging leaders with younger, better-educated ones. Deng has also made use of free-market forces to energize the economy. The reforms have moved at an uneven pace, and opponents of liberalization showed their muscle in 1987 by removing a key supporter, Hu Yaobang, the general secretary of the Communist party. By late 1987 the pace of change appeared to have stalled, as leaders jockeyed for power to succeed Deng.

China's foreign policy entered a more active phase after Mao's death. China has joined a number of regional and multilateral organizations, including the Asian Development Bank, and has applied to join the General Agreement on Tariffs and Trade (GATT).

China refuses to rule out the use of force in reunifying Taiwan with the mainland. Deng's solution is based on the idea of "one country, two systems" that China plans to apply in the case of Hong Kong.

Since 1982, Chinese and Soviet officials have met to discuss a normalization of relations. China cites three obstacles: the presence of Soviet armed forces on the common border and in Mongolia; Soviet troops in Afghanistan; and Vietnam's occupation of Cambodia (Kampuchea). If the Soviet Union completes its pullout from Afghanistan, that will eliminate one obstacle. If Vietnam carries out the promised withdrawal of 50,000 troops and places the remaining 75,000 under Cambodian command, China might be pressured to agree to the first Sino-Soviet summit since 1959.

China's relations with the U.S.—which the PRC blames for preventing its reunification with Taiwan—have not been entirely smooth in recent years. China, which gains hard currency from arms sales, protested when the U.S. curbed high-technology exports in Oct. 1987 in retaliation for China's sale of Silkworm missiles to Iran. China has also objected to U.S. criticism of its human rights record, including the repression of dissent in Tibet, and of its family planning program. It resents continued U.S. arms sales to Taiwan, which amounted to some $800 million in fiscal year 1988.

Taiwan has been ruled for 40 years by the Nationalist (Kuomintang) party, led by Chiang Kai-shek until his death in 1975. Chiang's son, Chiang Ching-kuo, succeeded him and, after his death in Jan. 1988, was replaced by a native Taiwanese, Lee Teng-hui. The authoritarian government has provided stability and successfully transformed an agricultural economy into a dynamic industrial one. An opposition party was formed in Sept. 1986, which prompted the government to institute reforms intended to modernize and democratize the political system. Martial law, in effect for four decades, ended in 1987. Still, the government exercises close control through a new national security law. Native Taiwanese, who constitute 85% of the population, hold less than 15% of the seats in national legislative bodies.

The major question facing Taiwan is its future relationship with mainland China. All contacts with the PRC were long proscribed, but this is changing. There is great public interest in China, and visits to the mainland are allowed.

Although the U.S. severed diplomatic ties with Taiwan in 1979, it continues to have close military and economic links. Under the terms of the Aug. 17, 1982, communiqué, the U.S. made a commitment to the PRC to "reduce gradually" arms sales to Taiwan, but no date was set for their termination. This commitment was implicitly tied to China's pursuit of a peaceful resolution of the Taiwan issue. The U.S., Taiwan's main trading partner, buys half of Taiwan's exports, which has led to large surpluses in Taiwan's trade with the U.S. ($16 billion in 1987). Taiwan's main fear, like that of other East Asian countries with strong economies, is U.S. protectionism.

With the exception of the U.S. connection, Taiwan is diplomatically isolated. This could change if the PRC accepts Taiwan's formula of "dual recognition," allowing countries to recognize both Chinese governments.

U.S. RELATIONS

For three decades, U.S. policy toward mainland China was based on nonrecognition, military containment and economic embargo. Until 1971, the U.S. managed to prevent the PRC from replacing Taiwan as China's representative at the United Nations. Taiwan enjoyed not only U.S. diplomatic support but a defense commitment which was critical to its survival.

By the early 1970s, the stage was set for a Sino-American rapprochement. A thaw in relations with the U.S. could provide China with a counterweight to a hostile Soviet Union. For the U.S., a warming of relations with the PRC could increase Washington's leverage with Moscow and spur a negotiated settlement of the war in Vietnam.

President Richard M. Nixon's 1972 visit to China set the stage for normalization. At the conclusion of his trip he acknowledged that "all

Chinese on either side of the Taiwan Strait maintain there is but one China and that Taiwan is a part of China." But it was not until Dec. 1978 that the U.S. recognized Beijing as the sole legal government of China and broke diplomatic ties with Taiwan, effective Jan. 1, 1979. The U.S. terminated its mutual defense treaty a year later. The U.S. has insisted that China resolve its dispute with Taiwan peacefully.

The Taiwan Relations Act of Apr. 1979 established a legal framework for U.S. relations with Taiwan. The U.S. embassy in Taiwan's capital, Taipei, was replaced by a nongovernmental entity, the American Institute in Taiwan, and the Taiwanese embassy in the U.S. was replaced by the Coordination Council for North American Affairs. Substantial trade, including the sale of U.S. arms "sufficient" for Taiwan's defense, continues between the two countries and remains a major obstacle to better Sino-American relations.

ADMINISTRATION POLICY

The Reagan Administration has had to balance its security and economic interests in formulating policy toward China and Taiwan. The U.S. seeks to maintain friendly relations with both countries, guarantee Taiwan's ability to defend itself, and encourage the two governments to reconcile their differences without U.S. involvement.

Since normalizing relations, top American and Chinese leaders have exchanged visits and concluded many scientific, technological and cultural agreements. Outstanding private claims have been resolved and a trade agreement has been concluded. China is the 16th largest U.S. trade partner, with two-way trade in 1986 totaling over $8 billion. Some 250,000 American tourists visit China annually.

Since 1981, China allegedly has provided the U.S. with intelligence facilities near the Soviet border. The U.S. has approved selected military sales and technology transfers. The U.S. offers China nuclear cooperation as well, even though the Department of Defense lists China as a nation hostile to the U.S.

The most serious Administration concern with Beijing at present is the latter's selling of missiles to Iran and Saudi Arabia.

In 1987 China was the largest supplier of textiles to the U.S. Under American pressure, China agreed in Dec. 1987 to restrain the growth of textile exports to 3% annually through 1991.

The U.S. recognizes Chinese sovereignty over Tibet but has expressed concern over the suppression of anti-Chinese demonstrations that have taken place there since Oct. 1987.

The major source of friction between the Administration and Taiwan is the trade imbalance. U.S. industry wants greater access to Taiwan's market.

POLICY CHOICES

❏ The U.S. should strengthen economic and defense ties with the PRC.
Yes. (1) China makes a vital contribution to U.S.

Current History, Inc.

The People's Republic of China

strategic interests by serving as a counterweight to Soviet influence in Asia. (2) China, as it modernizes, will become an increasingly important market for U.S. products and services.
No. (1) China is a Communist country that is politically unstable and economically backward. (2) China protects its domestic market, and the obstacles to profitable participation by U.S. companies are legion.

❐ The U.S. should give priority to maintaining economic and defense ties with Taiwan.
Yes. (1) Taiwan is an ally of long standing that continues to support Western security goals, and the U.S. should not abandon it. (2) Taiwan is a major U.S. trade partner.
No. (1) Taiwan is powerful, but it does not control the mainland. The PRC does and therefore the U.S. must deal with it. (2) As long as the U.S. continues its support, Taiwan will delay a peaceful resolution of its differences with the PRC.

SELECT BIBLIOGRAPHY

"China: Reform and Future Prospects." *Department of State Bulletin,* Dec. 1987, pp. 51–54. U.S. view of bilateral relations.

Ching, Frank, *Hong Kong and China: For Better or For Worse.* New York, Foreign Policy Association, 1985. Prospects for the transition of power.

Goldstein, Steven M., and Mathews, Jay, "Sino-American Relations After Normalization: Toward the Second Decade." *Headline Series* No. 276. New York, Foreign Policy Association, Nov./Dec. 1985. Key issues affecting future relations.

Harrison, Selig S., "Taiwan After Chiang Ching-kuo." *Foreign Affairs,* Spring 1988, pp. 790–808. Examines political transition.

17

Japan: Economic Colossus

✔ *Can the U.S. successfully compete with Japan?*
✔ *What are major causes of the trade imbalance?*
✔ *Should Japan assume a greater role in its own defense?*

The countries compared:	Japan	U.S.
Population	122 mil.	244 mil.
Per capita GNP (1987)	$19,642	$18,411
Average GNP growth (1973–86)	4.3%	2.5%
Balance of payments (1987)	+$87 bil.	–$161 bil.
Exports to the U.S./Japan	$88 bil.	$28 bil.

FACTS

- Japan is the principal U.S. ally in East Asia; there are 55,000 U.S. troops in Japan.
- The U.S. spent 6.5% of its gross national product (GNP) on defense in 1987; Japan spent about 1%.
- Japan has the fifth largest defense budget in the world.
- Japan is the largest U.S. trade partner after Canada; the U.S. is Japan's largest trade partner.
- The U.S. trade deficit in 1987 amounted to $171 billion, of which $60 billion was with Japan.

BACKGROUND

Political development. After defeating Japan in World War II, the U.S. occupied it for nearly seven years and introduced far-reaching changes. Under the Constitution of 1947, Japan became a parliamentary democracy. By law Japan cannot maintain military forces. (The role of the Self-Defense Force, or SDF, is limited to protection of the homeland.)

In 1952 Japan's sovereignty was restored, and a bilateral security agreement granted the U.S. base rights. The 1960 Treaty of Mutual Cooperation and Security, which is still in effect, commits the U.S. to defend Japan, although Japan is not obliged to defend the U.S.

Japan has been governed since 1955 by the Liberal Democratic party (LDP), which has provided extraordinary stability and prosperity. The LDP has been led since Nov. 1987 by Prime Minister Noboru Takeshita. He is expected to continue the policies of Yasuhiro Nakasone (1982–87), which were aimed at strengthening Japanese-U.S. security relations and promoting domestic growth.

Economic miracle. Japan is heavily dependent on foreign trade. The country must import 80% to 100% of the raw materials it needs, including all its petroleum and much of its food. The country owes much of its early economic success to government protection of industry and market intervention. A well-educated, disciplined labor force with a strong work ethic was also beneficial. Japan was initially successful in producing steel, chemicals and ships; the emphasis later shifted to plastics, automobiles and electronics. Agriculture is the weakest and most protected sector of the economy.

Trade barriers. Japan's ability to import depends on its foreign exchange earnings, which helps account for its "export at any cost" ethic and its protectionist policies. The principal obstacles to foreign exporters are nontariff barriers, including restrictive business practices, burdensome customs procedures and quotas. U.S. producers have also found it difficult to overcome supplier loyalty, rigid quality standards and a labyrinthine distribution system.

On the other hand, Japan has the lowest average import tariffs among the major industrialized countries and has voluntarily restrained exports of automobiles, televisions, textiles and steel.

Defense. Since World War II, Japan has refused to permit the introduction of nuclear weapons on its soil, although U.S. warships visiting Japan are assumed to be nuclear-armed.

Defense spending and the size of the SDF have been strictly limited. The SDF has a ceiling of 250,000 personnel, and until Jan. 1987 defense expenditures were held to no more than 1% of GNP. Only very modest increases are expected.

Largely in response to U.S. pressure, Japan has assumed some responsibility for regional security, including protecting its sea-lanes out to 1,000 nautical miles. Japan has also been increasing its contribution ($2.5 billion in 1988) toward the support of U.S. troops based in Japan.

Foreign affairs. The Japanese consider themselves a people apart, isolated and extremely vulnerable to economic shocks, such as an oil cutoff. They resent U.S. pressure to reduce the bilateral trade imbalance and believe that Washington is looking to Tokyo to solve American problems, including a lack of product competitiveness and an unwillingness to balance the Federal budget. At the same time, the American and Japanese economies have become extensively interdependent, and Japan recognizes that it must make an effort to placate the U.S.

Japan has a huge financial stake in the U.S. economy. Japanese at first invested in U.S. Treasury bonds and corporate securities, later in real estate, and are now buying U.S. companies. Japan wants access to American technology and has invested heavily in U.S. manufacturing, especially autos. Some 100,000 Americans work in Japanese-owned manufacturing plants. This has raised the question of whether so large a Japanese stake in the U.S. economy is healthy.

On most foreign policy issues Japan has followed the U.S. lead. Although increased Japanese military spending would help relieve the U.S. burden of protecting the Pacific, it is opposed by Japan's neighbors, especially China and the members of the Association of Southeast Asian Nations (ASEAN), which suffered under Japanese occupation during World War II.

Foreign aid. Today Japan has the second largest foreign aid program in the world and helps advance U.S. policy goals at a time when U.S. aid funds are being reduced. Japan budgeted over $9 billion in development assistance for the year beginning Apr. 1, 1988.

ADMINISTRATION POLICY

The Administration is concerned with the huge U.S. trade deficit with Japan. Despite voluntary attempts by Japan to restrain them, exports to the U.S. increased 3.9% in 1987. Japanese automobiles and car parts, which account for more than one third of Japanese exports to the U.S., are a symbol of mutual antagonism.

The U.S. wants Japan to remove trade barriers, liberalize its financial markets and increase imports. The U.S. ambassador to Japan, Mike Mansfield, believes what is needed most is a comprehensive trade agreement with Japan.

The exchange rate now benefits U.S. exporters. The appreciation of the yen against the dollar, which began in Sept. 1985, contributed in 1987 to the first decrease in Japan's trade surplus in five years. (In 1985 it took 260 yen to buy a dollar; in May 1988 it took 125.)

Despite the strengthening of bilateral security relations and Japan's participation in research for the U.S. Strategic Defense Initiative, the overall climate of trust appears to have seriously eroded. In Apr. 1987 President Ronald Reagan imposed the first trade sanctions against Japan since World War II because it sold microchips below cost in third-country markets in violation of a 1986 agreement. Another major storm erupted when it was revealed that the Toshiba Co. had sold militarily useful technology to the Soviet Union, compromising the U.S. ability to track Soviet submarines. A major sticking point at present is Japanese restrictions on U.S. beef and citrus products.

Critics charge that the U.S. lacks a strategy for trading with Japan. "U.S. behavior toward Japan is eccentric, episodic and devoid of any long-term vision of where this important relationship should be headed and how it will get there," according to George R. Packard of the School of Advanced International Studies of The Johns Hopkins University. Critics also fault U.S. trade negotiators for misunderstanding the Japanese and emphasizing short-term relief rather than long-term planning.

POLICY CHOICES

❏ The U.S. should insist that Japan relax trade barriers.
Yes. (1) Japan's surplus with the U.S. is partly due to its unfair trade practices. (2) Past pressure has resulted in some accommodation to U.S. concerns; greater pressure might produce greater results.
No. (1) Japan's trade barriers only affect a small percentage of U.S. exports to that country. (2) The U.S. should recognize that internal constraints prevent Japan from significantly increasing imports from the U.S.

❏ The U.S. should take steps to reduce imports from Japan.
Yes. (1) By curbing Japanese imports, the U.S. will protect its own industries. (2) Reducing Japa-

nese imports is essential to reduce the U.S. trade deficit.
No. (1) Penalizing imports from Japan would lead to higher prices for the U.S. consumer. (2) Japan would retaliate by erecting additional barriers to U.S. imports, resulting in an even higher U.S. trade deficit.

☐ **The U.S. should urge Japan to increase its contribution to international security.**
Yes. Japan can afford to increase its economic aid to Third World countries (such as the Philippines) that support Western security goals. This would lighten the U.S. foreign aid burden.
No. Japan has already increased its foreign aid budget. Japan's foreign aid priorities must be determined by Japan, not the U.S.

SELECT BIBLIOGRAPHY

"Japan, 1988." *Current History,* Apr. 1988 (entire issue). A survey by eight experts.

Packard, George R., "The Coming U.S.-Japan Crisis." *Foreign Affairs,* Winter 1987/88, pp. 348–67. Recommends a commission of "wise men" to guide future bilateral relations.

Pempel, T.J., "Japan: The Dilemmas of Success." *Headline Series* No. 277. New York, Foreign Policy Association, Jan./Feb. 1986. An illuminating portrait.

Reischauer, Edwin O., *The Japanese Today: Change and Continuity.* Cambridge, Mass., Harvard University Press, 1988. An updated classic.

Sigur, Gaston J., Jr., "Current Reflections on U.S.-Japan Relations." *Department of State Bulletin,* May 1988, pp. 31–33. Overview by U.S. diplomat.

"A Survey of Japan." *The Economist* (London), Dec. 5, 1987. Profile of Japan, focusing on the economy.

18

The U.S. and the UN

✔ *Is the UN still relevant?*
✔ *Should the U.S. restore its full contribution?*
✔ *Should the U.S. call for a reduced assessment?*

FACTS

- **United Nations Charter** was signed in 1945 at San Francisco Conference by 50 nations.
- **Current membership:** 159.
- **Principal organs** established under UN Charter include: General Assembly (all members, each with one vote); Security Council (15 members, including 5 permanent members with veto power—U.S., U.S.S.R., Britain, France, China); Economic and Social Council (54 members); International Court of Justice, known as World Court (15 judges).
- **Specialized agencies** include Food and Agriculture Organization (FAO), International Labor Organization (ILO), World Health Organization (WHO), UN Educational, Scientific and Cultural Organization (UNESCO), International Bank for Reconstruction and Development (IBRD or World Bank) and its affiliates, the International Development Association (IDA) and International Finance Corporation (IFC).
- **The secretariat** in New York City is the UN's administrative arm, which carries out programs and policies established by UN organs.

- **The secretary-general,** the UN's chief administrative officer (now serving his second term, which ends in 1992), is Javier Pérez de Cuéllar of Peru.
- **Budget:**
  - UN regular budget for two years, 1988–89: $1.77 billion.
  - Total arrears owed to UN (at end of 1987): $353.4 million, of which the U.S. owes $252.8 million.
  - U.S. assessment for 1987: $212.9 million (25% of total UN regular budget), of which the U.S. paid $100 million. Restoration of $44 million more is pending in Congress.
  - U.S. assessment for 1988: $214.9 million. Administration request for 1988: $144 million.

BACKGROUND

The UN Charter, adopted in the closing months of World War II, called for the peaceful resolution of international conflicts and the growth of worldwide material prosperity. It envisaged U.S.-Soviet cooperation in maintaining the peace. **The cold war** between the U.S. and U.S.S.R. undermined the short-lived East-West consensus. The first issue raised in the Security Council in 1946 was Moscow's refusal to withdraw its troops from Iran. The rift widened with the Korean War (1950–53).

Decolonization in the late 1950s and early 1960s led to a substantial increase in membership. These newly independent nations often challenged U.S. positions, usually joining the Soviet bloc to form a two-thirds majority in the General Assembly, ending the era of almost automatic majorities in favor of the U.S. In 1964, the developing nations formed an economic caucus, the Group of 77 (now numbering 125), which represents their desire for a greater share of world resources and more trade and aid.

The Nonaligned Movement, which began formal meetings in 1961 in an attempt to give the Third World a unified political voice, is a cohesive but not monolithic bloc of 101 nations. Other voting blocs include the Warsaw Pact (the Soviet-East European alliance), the African Group and the Islamic Conference. The U.S. tends to be in the minority on most questions concerning the Middle East and southern Africa but has enjoyed majority support on key resolutions on Afghanistan and Cambodia (Kampuchea).

The State Department has submitted an annual report to Congress since 1985 on voting practices in the UN. While the U.S. remains isolated in opposition to many General Assembly resolutions, the 1988 report concludes that "in general, many key U.S. foreign policy interests fared well" and that name-calling targeted at the U.S. has all but disappeared in General Assembly resolutions on controversial topics. On the other hand, the report noted that UN members' overall support for the U.S. continued to fall, although it is higher on major issues of importance to the U.S.

Budget. The UN regular budget covers administrative expenses of principal UN organs, but not the specialized agencies. The UN Development Program (UNDP), the UN Office of High Commissioner for Refugees (UNHCR), and the UN Children's Fund (UNICEF), among others, are funded on a voluntary basis. Additional assessments may be levied for peacekeeping forces, such as the UN Interim Force in Lebanon, UNIFIL. (The UN Force in Cyprus is financed by voluntary contributions.)

Crisis. U.S. dissatisfaction with the UN during the 1970s over what it saw as anti-Western bias in UN decisions stimulated congressional criticism of UN budget growth and bureaucratic inefficiency. Sen. Nancy Landon Kassebaum (R-Kans.) successfully sponsored legislation that threatened a one-fifth reduction in U.S. dues payments if the UN did not adopt a system of weighted voting on budgetary matters. Despite protests in the U.S. and abroad that the measure was a flagrant violation of the treaty obligation to pay assessments as spelled out in the UN Charter, the Kassebaum Amendment went into effect on Oct. 1, 1986. In combination with budgetary measures to reduce the size of the U.S. Federal deficit and other pressures, the end result was that the U.S. paid only $100 million of its 1986 assessment of over $200 million, bringing the UN very close to bankruptcy.

Fiscal reform. In anticipation of a significant shortfall in the U.S. contribution for 1986, the secretary-general had already taken drastic steps early in the year to curtail spending. He imposed a hiring freeze, froze salaries, cut back on official travel, halted construction and called for other economies that saved over $80 million (11% of the net budget).

That year, the UN also appointed the "Group of 18" to develop recommendations for fiscal reform. The resulting resolution, adopted in Dec. 1986, established a new budgeting procedure and created the 21-member Committee for Programming and Coordination to implement it. The new procedure implicitly recognizes the U.S. demand for weighted voting on budgetary matters by mandating that the budget be adopted by "consensus" in the committee—i.e. without a vote—before being sent to the General Assembly, thus giving the U.S. an unofficial veto on spending measures. The resolution also called for a 15% reduction in UN staff (25% at the most senior levels), provided for supplemental emergency funds, and suggested ways to restructure and streamline the bureaucracy.

The Reagan Administration praised the reform agreement as "historic," and promised its "best efforts" to persuade Congress to restore full funding of the U.S. assessment in 1987. But deficit pressures and skepticism in Congress combined to produce an appropriation for 1987 that was $60 million short of the assessment. Even close U.S. allies complained that Washington was reneging on its end of the bargain, and the 21-member committee failed to agree on the 1988–89 budget. Nevertheless, the budget of $1.77 billion passed by the General Assembly is the first in many years to represent negative growth in real terms (taking account of inflation). It was also the first in a long time to receive near-unanimous support: all but four General Assembly member states voted in its favor.

Reform progress. The UN has achieved significant economies, having reduced spending by roughly $113.6 million in 1986 and 1987. As of Dec. 17, 1987, 89 members were in arrears, 39 of whom owed more than one year's assessment.

There has been talk in the UN of reducing the U.S. assessment rate to something that Congress could support. The fact that the U.S. paid no more in 1987 than it did in 1986, despite the reform agreement, has intensified speculation about the need to reduce the U.S. rate from 25% to 20%, 15%, or even 10% of the total. Secretary of State George P. Shultz testified before a Senate subcommittee in Apr. 1988 that the Administration would be giving careful consideration to this matter this year.

Role redefinition? The UN Charter was written before the advent of nuclear weapons, the East-West conflict and the North-South divisions that followed decolonization—events that deeply affected the UN's capacity to fulfill its role as international peacekeeper. The most successful peacekeeping operation was in the former Belgian Congo, now Zaire, in 1960–64, when 20,000 UN troops helped save the new nation from being recolonized or partitioned by pro-Soviet and pro-Belgian factions and also prevented a threatened U.S.-Soviet clash in Africa. UN forces have also served the cause of peace in Korea, Cyprus and the Middle East. The UN has been least successful when there has been disagreement among the Security Council's permanent members—especially the superpowers—who must approve all peacekeeping operations.

A new Soviet role? An important factor in strengthening the UN may be the recent change in the Soviet attitude toward international organizations. Soviet leader Mikhail Gorbachev has spoken out in favor of using the UN to resolve regional disputes and backed up his rhetoric by paying a portion of the $225 million debt owed to the UN for regular dues and peacekeeping operations. The more the superpowers can agree to work together on common interests at the UN, as they did in July 1987 when the Security Council voted unanimously for a cease-fire in the Iran-Iraq War, the more effective the UN is likely to be.

In other areas, the UN has done best on issues where large numbers of nations were persuaded that lack of agreement threatened all their interests. The 1987 agreement to stop production of ozone-depleting chemicals is one example. Another is the UN action against terrorism: after years of North-South argument over whether terrorists should be prosecuted regardless of their motives, or whether the causes of terrorism—poverty and discrimination—should be eliminated first, the General Assembly in 1985 passed a resolution denouncing all terrorist acts as criminal. The UN also sponsored the six-year peace talks between Afghanistan and Pakistan that led to the Soviet withdrawal from Afghanistan beginning in May 1988 (see Chapter 12).

Operating away from the political spotlight, many of the **specialized agencies** have made important contributions. These include the WHO AIDS control program and the International Atomic Energy Agency's (IAEA) proposal for an expanded safeguards system against the proliferation of nuclear weapons.

ADMINISTRATION POLICY

The Reagan Administration welcomed the UN's fiscal reforms but has been internally divided over how much priority to attach to restoration of funding. Legislation was passed in Dec. 1987 modifying the Kassebaum Amendment and thereby opening the door to a return to full funding, subject to successful implementation of UN reform. But the agreement came too late to make a difference in 1987, and continued debate over the success of UN reform makes the 1988 payment look uncertain.

Congress has usually appropriated significantly more for UN voluntary programs, such as UNICEF and UNDP, than the Administration has requested.

In addition to withholding funds, the U.S. has taken other actions to retaliate against perceived anti-American bias. The U.S. withdrew from UNESCO in Dec. 1984, for example, charging that the agency had become politicized and hostile to the U.S., and that it had mismanaged funds.

POLICY OPTIONS

❐ The U.S. should restore its full contribution to the UN.
Yes. (1) Full payment of its UN assessments is a legal obligation of the U.S. as spelled out in the UN Charter. (2) Payment would help bring about a major policy objective: maximum UN reform. (3) Given the recent Soviet interest in the UN, the U.S. should remain actively engaged.
No. (1) The best lever the U.S. has to control waste and inefficiency in the UN is partial withholding of its assessment. (2) The UN's performance on reform so far has been inadequate, and economic pressure should be maintained. (3) Full funding for the UN in an age of tight U.S. budgets takes away funds from other pressing U.S. needs.

❐ The U.S. should call for a reduced assessment.
Yes. (1) The U.S. does not have enough confidence in the UN to justify carrying a 25% share of its cost. (2) It is not healthy for the UN to depend so

heavily on one member state. (3) Congress appears unwilling to vote appropriations at the 25% level, so the only practical course is to reduce the assessment.

No. (1) As more problems become global in scope, the U.S. will have greater need of the UN to work out solutions and will therefore need a strong presence there. (2) The 25% level corresponds roughly to the U.S. share of world gross national product. (3) A reduction would signal a decline in U.S. influence in the world.

SELECT BIBLIOGRAPHY

Gardner, Richard N., "Practical Internationalism." *Foreign Affairs,* Spring 1988, pp. 827–45. Urges a strengthening of international institutions and an active American role in them.

Kirkpatrick, Jeane J., "Projecting and Protecting U.S. Interests in the United Nations." *Vital Speeches of the Day,* Feb. 1, 1988, pp. 226–30. Address by former ambassador to the UN.

Krauthammer, Charles, "Let It Sink." *The New Republic,* Aug. 24, 1987, pp. 18–23. Why the U.S. shouldn't bail out the UN.

Laurenti, Jeffrey, *A Stronger Hand: Shaping an American Agenda for a More Effective United Nations.* New York, The United Nations Association of the U.S.A., 1988. Briefing book covers U.S. interests and UN role on major issues.

Reagan, Ronald, "America's Vision of the Future." *Department of State Bulletin,* Nov. 1987, pp. 1–4. President's address before the General Assembly.

INDEX

A

ABM. See antiballistic missile.
"accidents measures" agreement, 13
acid rain, 121–122, 123
Afghanistan, 34, 58, 79, 82, 104, 106, 115, 149, 152
Africa, southern, 84–92
Africa, sub-Saharan, 51, 52
African National Congress, 88, 90, 91
Agency for International Development (AID), 53, 54
agriculture, 43, 45, 52, 55, 94
  exports, foreign, 49, 52, 64
aid: 48–56, 66, 67, 70, 71, 88, 90, 104, 105, 107
aircraft, 18, 98, 105, 115
ANC. See African National Congress.
Angola, 34, 84, 85, 88, 89, 90
antiballistic missile systems, treaty on, 13, 15, 111
antisatellite weapon, 23, 26, 29
apartheid, 85, 86, 88, 89
Arab-Israeli wars: 33, 74, 95
  peace plans, 75–77, 79–80
Arab nationalism, 74, 81
Arafat, Yasir, 78
Argentina, 50, 129
Arias Sánchez, Oscar, 64, 68, 71
arms:
  conventional, 16–18, 23, 25, 97, 98
  nuclear, 26–27, 94
  sales, 81, 136, 138, 139
  strategic, 13–16, 23, 25, 26, 27, 98
  tactical, 18, 98
arms control, 12–21, 22, 96, 111, 112
ASAT. See antisatellite weapon.
Atlantic Alliance. See North Atlantic Treaty Organization.
"Atlantic-to-Urals" agreement, 16–18
automobiles, 44, 118, 120, 142, 144
Azcona Hoyo, José, 66

B

Baker, James A., 3d: 43, 54
  Baker Plan, 53, 129
Bangladesh, 102
Belgium, 93, 98
Belize, 58, 64
Bhutto, Benazir, 102
birthrates, 50, 51
Boland Amendment, 7
bombers, 16, 22, 23, 25, 27, 105
Botha, P.W., 86, 87
Botswana, 85, 88
Bracero Program, 128
Brazil, 50, 129
Bretton Woods, 40
Brezhnev, Leonid I., 14, 111
Britain, 17, 36, 43, 73, 74, 77, 84, 93, 94, 98, 102, 147
budget cuts: 28–29, 53
  impact of, 7, 22, 24–25, 61, 98–99
budget deficit, 9, 22, 43, 44, 96, 150
Bulgaria, 17, 109

C

Cambodia, 136, 149
Camp David, 76
Canada, 43, 45, 93, 118–124, 141
Carlucci, Frank C., 28–29
Carter, Jimmy, 9, 67, 75–76, 106, 111
  Carter Doctrine, 79
Central America, 7, 52, 63–72, 115, 131
Central Intelligence Agency, 5, 6, 34, 65
Central Treaty Organization (CENTO), 74, 104
Cerezo Arévalo, Marco Vinicio, 65
chemical weapons, 96
Chiang Ching-kuo, 136
Chiang Kai-shek, 136
China, People's Republic of, 50, 51, 54, 57, 77, 82, 103, 104, 113, 134–140, 144, 147
CIA. See Central Intelligence Agency.
Clark Amendment, 89
Clean Air Act of 1970, 121
cold war, 109–111, 148
Colombia, 57, 58, 64, 131
commodities, 49, 54, 64
Common Market. See EEC.
Conference on Disarmament in Europe (CDE), 16, 17
Conference on Security and Cooperation in Europe (CSCE), 111
Congress: 5–8, 14, 15, 22, 45, 61, 67, 70, 81, 87, 89, 105, 107, 121, 130, 149, 150, 153
  funding of programs, 28–29, 61, 67, 70, 81, 105, 121, 150, 153
  ratification of treaties, 14, 111, 118, 120
constructive engagement, 89–90
Contadora Group, 64, 131, 132
contras, 7, 64, 66–70
Costa Rica, 59, 64, 68
Cuba, 34, 64, 89, 90, 111
Cyprus, 149, 151

D

debt: 63, 68, 134
  crisis, 50, 54, 125, 128–129
  Federal, 39, 42
  Morgan plan, 129, 131
  service, 50
defense (U.S.), 22–31, 98–99, 119
Delvalle Henríquez, Eric Arturo, 69
Deng Xiaoping, 135
Denmark, 17, 93
détente, 95, 111
developed countries, 48
development, 50–52
devolution, 97–98
"Discriminate Deterrence," 25
disengagement, 98
disinvestment, 88
dollar, U.S., 41, 43, 96, 144
drug traffic, 57–62, 69, 70, 125, 128, 130–131, 132
dual track, 96
Duarte, José Napoleón, 66

E

EC (European Community), 87
EEC (European Economic Community), 94, 96
Egypt, 52, 53, 74–78, 80
El Salvador, 35, 63, 64, 65–66, 69, 70
emigration, 112, 115, 116, 126, 128
exports: 39–40, 42, 48, 49, 64, 118–119, 125, 126, 130, 141, 142–143, 144
  quotas, 44

F

family planning, 51, 54–55, 136
Finland, 33, 111
flexible response, 96
food: 51–52, 55
  Food for Peace, 55
Ford, Gerald R., 14, 106
foreign aid. See aid.
foreign investment, 44, 119, 120, 143–144
Foreign Investment Review Agency, 119
France, 17, 43, 73, 74, 77, 93, 94, 98, 147
free trade agreement (FTA), 45, 114, 120–121, 132

G

Gandhi, Rajiv, 102–103, 106–107
Galvin, John, 93
Gaza, 74, 76, 77
General Agreement on Tariffs and Trade (GATT), 40–41, 130, 135
Geneva accord of 1988, 106, 115
Germany (West), 9, 33, 35, 39, 43, 93, 94, 98
glasnost, 112
Golan Heights, 74
gold standard, 40–41
Gorbachev, Mikhail, 15, 16, 96, 109, 111–117, 152
Gramm-Rudman-Hollings, 7
Greece, 9, 53, 93
Group of 5, 43
Group of 7, 43
Group of 77, 148
GSP (Generalized System of Preferences), 54
Guatemala, 63, 65
Guatemala accord, 64, 66, 67, 70, 131, 132

H

Helsinki agreement, 111
Honduras, 59, 64, 66, 67, 70
Hong Kong, 51, 135
hostages, in Lebanon, 8, 36
"hot-line" accord, 13
Hu Yaobang, 135
human rights, 65, 66, 69, 115, 136
Hungary, 17, 109
Hussein, King, 77, 80

I

ICBM. See intercontinental ballistic missile.
Iceland, 15, 93, 96
immigration, 128, 132
Immigration Reform and Control Act, 128
imports: 48, 87, 118–119, 125, 130, 132, 141
  quotas, 44
India, 50, 84, 101–108
INF. See intermediate-range nuclear forces.
intercontinental ballistic missile, 14, 15–16, 25
interest rates, 49, 96
interim agreement on the limitation of strategic offensive arms, 13
intermediate-range nuclear forces: 96
  treaty, 8, 14, 15, 19, 96, 112
International Atomic Energy Agency (IAEA), 152
International Monetary Fund (IMF), 53, 126
Investment Canada Act, 119
Iran, 34, 36, 74, 78–79, 80–81, 82, 104, 136, 139, 148
Iran-contra affair, 7–8, 36, 67, 80
Iran-Iraq War, 73, 79, 80, 81, 152
Iraq, 74, 79, 80, 81–82
Irish Republican Army, Provisional (IRA), 33, 34
Islamic Conference, 149
Israel, 35, 52, 53, 73, 74–78, 79, 80, 95, 113
Italy, 17, 36, 73, 93, 98

J

Jackson-Vanik Amendment, 116
Japan, 9, 36, 40, 43, 44, 113, 141–146
Joint Chiefs of Staff, 5–6, 19, 23, 98, 99
Jordan, 74, 76, 77, 79, 80

K

Kampuchea. See Cambodia.
Kashmir, 103
Kassebaum Amendment, 149–150, 153
Khan, Ayub, 102
Khan, Yahya, 102
Khomeini, Ayatollah Ruhollah, 79
Kissinger, Henry A., 75
Korean War, 111, 148
Kuwait, 35, 81

L

Laos, 58, 61
LDC (less-developed country). See Third World.
Lebanon, 8, 35, 36, 80, 149
Lee Teng-hui, 136
Lesotho, 85, 88
Libya: 35
  terrorism, 34, 35, 36
limited test ban treaty, 13
Luxembourg, 93, 98

M

Madrid Hurtado, Miguel de la, 127, 131

Index

Malawi, 85, 88
Mansfield, Mike, 144
Mao Zedong, 134–135
maquiladora, 130
Marshall Plan, 52
Mazatlán summit, 132
MBFR. See mutual and balanced force reductions.
McFarlane, Robert C., 8
Medellín cartel, 58
Mexico, 45, 49–50, 58, 60, 64, 125–133
Middle East, 73–83
military:
   aid, 7, 53, 64, 65, 66, 70
   bases, facilities, 9, 53, 81, 142
   U.S. commitments, 9, 94, 95, 98, 142
   U.S. Southern Command, 68
   U.S. troops, 61, 66, 68
MIRV. See multiple independently targetable reentry vehicle.
missiles, 16, 23, 25, 26, 27, 96
Mitterrand, François, 94
Moscow summit (1972), 111
Moscow summit (1988), 90
Mozambique, 34, 85, 88–89, 90
mujahideen, 34, 104, 105, 106
Mulroney, Brian, 118, 119, 120, 121, 122
multiple independently targetable reentry vehicle (MIRV), 14
mutual and balanced force reductions (MBFR), 16–18

N

Najibullah, 106
Nakasone, Yasuhiro, 142
Namibia, 84, 85, 89, 90
National Security Council (NSC), 5, 8, 67
National Security Decision Directive No. 138, 36
NATO. See North Atlantic Treaty Organization.
Navy, 23, 25, 29, 71, 81, 114
Netherlands, the, 93, 98
Nicaragua, 7, 63, 64, 66–67, 69, 70, 71, 80, 115, 128, 131
Nixon, Richard M.: 6, 111, 137
   Nixon Doctrine, 78
Nkomati Accord, 88–89
Nonaligned Movement, 105, 149
Noriega, Manuel Antonio, 58, 59, 68–69, 70
North. See developed countries.
North, Oliver L., 8
North American Aerospace Defense Command (NORAD), 122
North Atlantic Treaty Organization, 16–19, 81, 93–100, 109, 122
Norway, 17, 93
NSC. See National Security Council.
nuclear:
   India capability, 104
   nonproliferation treaty, 94
   "nuclear risk reduction centers" agreement, 14
   Pakistan program, 101
   technology trade, 123
   test ban, 14, 18
   weapons, 25, 94, 112, 122, 151

O

oil: 78, 79, 82, 95, 118, 125, 130, 142, 143
   dependence on, 73, 78, 95, 142
   prices, 49, 68, 82
omnibus trade bill, 45
on-site verification, 16, 114
Ortega Saavedra, Daniel, 67

P

Packard, George R., 3
Pakistan, 58, 74, 101–108, 152
Palestine Liberation Organization (PLO), 34, 77, 78
Palestinians, 76–78, 79
Panama, 58–59, 60, 64, 68–69, 70, 71, 131
peaceful nuclear explosions treaty, 14
Peres, Shimon, 77
perestroika, 112
Pérez de Cuellar, Javier, 148
Perkins, Edward J., 90
Persian Gulf, 73, 78–79, 80–81, 95
Peru, 57, 148
Philippines, 9, 52, 53
Pindling, Lynden O., 59
PLO. See Palestine Liberation Organization.
Poindexter, John M., 8
Poland, 109
Polar Sea, 123
population, 49, 50–51, 54–55, 63, 85, 100, 119, 125, 134, 141
Portugal, 9, 17, 53, 89, 93
protectionism, 40, 50, 96, 119, 120, 130, 142–143

R

Reagan, Ronald: 6, 15, 22, 44, 60, 66, 67, 79, 87, 96, 106, 107, 120, 121, 145
   Reagan Doctrine, 69, 90
   Reaganomics, 41
refugees, 104, 106
Renamo (Mozambique National Resistance), 34, 89
Resolution 242, 75
Reykjavik summit, 15, 96–97, 98
Romania, 17, 109

S

SADCC (South African Development Coordination Conference), 88, 90
Salinas de Gortari, Carlos, 127, 130, 131
SALT I, 13, 111
SALT II, 14, 111
Sandinistas, 7, 65, 66–70, 71, 80, 115, 128, 131
Saudi Arabia, 50, 139
scientific cooperation, 111, 115, 138
shah of Iran, 78, 105
Shamir, Yitzhak, 77, 78, 80

Shultz, George P., 8, 19, 90, 151
Sikhs, 102, 104
Silkworm missiles, 136
Sinai, 74, 76
skyjacking, 33, 34
SLBM. See submarine-launched ballistic missile.
Somoza family, 64, 67
South. See Third World.
South Africa, Union of, 84–92
South Korea, 9, 51
South-West Africa. See Namibia.
Soviet Union: 8, 12, 13–19, 22, 25, 64, 74, 77, 79, 90, 94, 95–96, 98, 103, 109–117, 136, 137, 145, 147, 148, 151, 152
   aid, 67, 89, 105, 135
   compliance with treaties, 14
   defense spending, 110, 114
   economic reforms, 112, 113
   emigration, 112
   invasion of Afghanistan, 79, 105, 136
   military aid, 67, 105
   nuclear weapons, 8, 12, 13–18
   pipeline dispute, 95
   submarines, 145
   test ban, unilateral, 18
   UN role, 77, 147, 152
Spain, 9, 17, 93
Sri Lanka, 104
SS-20 missiles, 96
Star Wars. See Strategic Defense Initiative.
Stark, U.S.S., 81–82
Stevenson Amendment, 116
stock market crash, 43, 96, 126, 127
Stockholm agreement, 16
strategic arms limitation talks. See SALT I and SALT II.
strategic arms reduction talks (START), 15, 19
Strategic Defense Initiative (SDI), 15, 19, 23, 25, 26, 144
submarine: 23, 122, 123, 145
   launched ballistic missile, 16, 23
SWAPO (South-West African People's Organization), 89
Swaziland, 85, 88
Syria, 34, 75, 79

T

Taiwan, 51, 134–140
Taiwan Relations Act, 138
Takeshita, Noboru, 142
Tambo, Oliver, 90
tanker war, 73, 81
Tanzania, 50, 85, 88
technology exchanges, 107, 113, 136, 138, 143, 145
terrorism, 32–38, 152
terrorists, negotiations with, 8, 35–36
textiles, exports to U.S., 49, 54, 139
Thailand, 58
Thatcher, Margaret, 94
Third World, 10, 48–56, 95, 111, 113–114, 128, 149
threshold test ban treaty, 14

Tibet, 136, 139
Tokyo summit, 36
Tower Commission, 8
trade: 39–47, 49, 50, 54, 73, 111, 113, 138
   barriers, 54, 142–143, 144
   deficit, 39, 42, 119, 141, 144
   direction of U.S. (chart), 42
   exports, U.S., 41, 49
   free trade, 40, 44, 113, 120–121, 130, 132
   imports, U.S., 41, 44, 49, 130, 132
   in services, 45, 120
   omnibus bill, 45
   sanctions, 87, 90–91, 145
   Soviet-U.S., 116
   tariffs, 45, 94, 143
   unfair practices, 43, 45
Treaty of Mutual Cooperation and Security, 142
Trudeau, Pierre Elliot, 118
Turkey, 9, 17, 52, 53, 74, 93

U

Unita (National Union for the Total Independence of Angola), 34, 89
United Nations: 137, 147–154
   Afghan peace plan, 106, 115
   funding, 148, 149, 150, 152
   peacekeeping operations, 76, 149, 151
   sanctions on South Africa, 85–86
   Security Council Resolution 435, 89
United Nations Children's Fund (UNICEF), 149, 153
United Nations Development Program (UNDP), 53, 149, 153
United Nations Educational, Scientific and Cultural Organization (UNESCO), 147, 153
United Nations Fund for Population Activities (UNFPA), 54

V

Vietnam: 136, 137
   War, 6, 61
Vladivostok summit, 14
Volcker, Paul, 43

W

War Powers Resolution, 6, 81
Warsaw Pact, 16–19, 97, 149
Weapons. See arms.
Webb, James H., Jr., 28, 29
Weinberger, Caspar W., 28, 29
West Bank, 74, 76, 77, 79, 80
Western European Union, 98
World Bank, 50, 53, 54, 56, 107, 147
World Health Organization (WHO), 147, 152
Wörner, Manfred, 93

Z

Zaire, 85
Zambia, 85, 88
Zia ul-Haq, 102
Zimbabwe, 85, 88

ORDER FORM

Send to *(please print)*

Name_____

Address_____

City_____ State_____ Zip_____

- **Prepayment must accompany every order of $8.00 or less, plus $1.50 for postage and handling.**

- Prepayment must accompany **all orders from individuals.** Please add postage and handling to your order as follows:

Orders up to $12.00	$1.50
Orders from $12.01–$30.00	$2.00
Orders from $30.01–$60.00	$3.00
Orders above $60.00	$5.00

- Educational institutions, businesses or libraries must prepay all orders of $8.00 or less, plus postage and handling. Larger orders can be billed if purchase order is received.

- **All orders outside the U.S.** and its possessions must be prepaid in **U.S. funds,** with a check drawn on a **U.S. correspondent bank.** Please include an *additional* $2.50 for postage.

- All bulk orders within the U.S. will be shipped U.P.S.

- Discounts: 10–99 ....25% off
  (For *Great Decisions* discounts, write or call FPA.)

- Please allow 3 to 4 weeks for delivery

    Mail to: Foreign Policy Association
                729 Seventh Avenue
                New York, N.Y. 10019

    or call: (212) 764–4050

(see reverse side)

Please send me:

_____ copies of *A Citizen's Guide to Foreign Policy: Election '88*
Price: $7.95 each

_____ copies of *Great Decisions 1988*
Price: $8.00 each

_____ copies of *Guide to Careers in World Affairs*
Price: $10.95 each

_____ copies of *Headline Series* No. 285, "The Shah, the Ayatollah and the U.S."

_____ copies of *Headline Series* No. 284, "Gorbachev's Foreign Policy"

_____ copies of *Headline Series* No. 283, "Global Television and Foreign Policy"

_____ copies of *Headline Series* No. 281, "Reforming the International Monetary System"

***Headline Series* price: $4.00 each**

Headline Series Subscriptions
(five issues per year)

❏ one year—$15.00

❏ two years—$25.00

❏ three years—$30.00

For subscriptions, please add

$3.00 *per year* for postage outside U.S.
$8.00 *per year* for first class mail outside U.S.

❏ *free* copy of FPA's Catalogue of Publications

(see reverse side)